SEVEN 7 SECRETS
OF A MEANINGFUL LIFE

FIND THE
MORE
YOU'VE BEEN
LOOKING
FOR

DAVID
HOUSHOLDER

BroadStreet
PUBLISHING

7 SECRETS OF A MEANINGFUL LIFE
FIND THE MORE YOU'VE BEEN LOOKING FOR

© 2014 by David Housholder

Published by BroadStreet Publishing
Racine, Wisconsin, USA
www.broadstreetpublishing.com

ISBN: 978-1-4245-4937-5 (hard cover)
ISBN: 978-1-4245-4950-4 (e-book)

Cover design by Garborg Design Works at www.garborgdesign.com
Interior design and typesetting by Katherine Lloyd at www.theDESKonline.com

Printed in China

14 15 16 17 18 19 20   7 6 5 4 3 2

7-20-2015

DEDICATION

To Wendy.
I only have eyes for you.

So you're thinking...

"Whatever... Another "Christian-ese" book.... like that's what I need? My child won't speak to me, my marriage is crumbing, I'm fat, and the mortgage is due every month until Jesus comes back. I've been there, done that religion thing—it doesn't work."

David Housholder knows this and so he writes about what it means to have a real and personal relationship with Jesus. Jesus who's in our everyday life, who knows, cares and loves us right where we're at. We can connect as Mr. Housholder shares with such insight, humor and practical real life scenarios.

Most importantly we find our connection to Christ Who gives us hope and meaning in the midst of our earthly experience challenges.

David writes:

"God thinks you're worth dying for. You are fearfully and wonderfully made, a miracle of biology and spirituality, full of dreams and visions. This self-graciousness will open up intimacy and friendship with others, and the heavens will start parting so that you can bask in the joy of the Lord."

"Okay, so sign me up!" Right!?

As I read the book I began to feel better because I started to "know" better. "Pastor Hous" will help you get there too as you learn who you are in Christ. He helps unlock the secrets for meaning and purpose in real and everyday life.

—Debbie Griffith
Radio Host, Everyday Matters
DebbieGriffith.com

WE ALL NEED TO KNOW THESE SECRETS! And not just know them but be able to make them our own. David has so masterfully taken God's passion for his children and put handles it for ANYONE who wants to really experience what living looks like.. As soon as you start reading you immediately become engaged saying "I can do this!" No more secrets!

—Peder Eide
Singer/Songwriter/Worship Leader
PederEide.com

Reading this book will be like talking with a church counselor. This isn't a stuffy, intellectual discussion of the nuances or historical theology: David Housholder tells story after story meant to remind you that life is far more than academic rigor. Life is spiritual. Each chapter stands alone, ready to offer up its own gift of wisdom. You could read this book in a day, but you probably shouldn't, since it demands reflection.

—J.F. Arnold
Editor in Chief, *Evangelical Outpost*
EvangelicalOutpost.com

My friend, David, has always had an HD view of life. He will introduce you to new colors, textures, and truths in the tapestry of life. Read this book for the SECRETS, but come away with the serenity of knowing a God who is with you and for you. Even now.

—Bill Bohline
Lead Pastor, Hosanna! (Minneapolis-St. Paul)
HosannaLC.org

In his latest book, Dave Housholder, gleans insights and wisdom from the Bible that have import for people living the abundant life God desires for them, and articulating them in such a way that help post-moderns grasp and understand them. He provides tools for reflection and discussion to help the reader process and apply the subject matter of each chapter. This book is a good resource for a small group, for discipling new believers, or to facilitate some authentic dialogue about the Christian faith with an interested seeker.

—Mike Bradley
Director, The Alliance of Renewal Churches (ARC)

David Housholder has written a devotional gem. The secrets he tells are indeed secrets to many. They are the well-known but so often neglected truths of Christian living. The centrality of knowing God, having a personal relationship with Jesus Christ, prayer, being present, and living with love, discipline, and joy are a few of these great secrets. But the book does more than present foundational spiritual disciplines. It inspires. It is engagingly written, well-illustrated and tells us how to practice these secrets. David tells of his own personal experiences and brings us "into the moment" with him while he tells us how to live faithfully "in the moment" with Christ.

—Dr. Robert B. Sloan, Jr.
President, Houston Baptist University
hbu.edu

The 7 Secrets offers a fresh perspective on life that includes some unpredictable wisdom for anyone interested in finding a better way.

—Mike Housholder
Senior Pastor, Lutheran Church of Hope
West Des Moines, Iowa
Largest mainline Protestant church in the US
HopeWDM.org

David is one of the guys I look to for ideas and insight. We all need his energy and example. Read this book.

—Mike Woodruff
Senior Pastor Christ Church of Lake Forest, IL
ChristchurchIL.org

These days most people don't know how to live, mainly because they never read the official instruction manual for life. With humor and refreshing honesty, David Housholder points us to the basic principles that make life meaningful. If you are looking for your life purpose, *The 7 Secrets* will help you find it!

—J. Lee Grady
Author of *Fearless Daughters of the Bible*

Light reading on heavy stuff. Housholder makes us think again how to live and love, with joy despite disappointments. A book for busy people of our time, as well as for those who take their time to think it all over.

—Willem B. Drees,
Editor of Zygon: Journal of Religion and Science, and professor of philosophy, Leiden and Tilburg, the Netherlands.

I have been on this planet for 69 years. I wish I had been exposed to these 7 Secrets 50 years ago, because they would have changed my life much earlier.

—Judge James P. Gray (Ret.)
Author of *A Voter's Handbook: Effective Solutions to America's Problems*

Once again David Housholder has masterfully brought together ancient wisdom and present-day practicality in a thoroughly accessible guide to a better life. Read this book and you will truly be blessed!

—Bob Rognlien
Author of *The Experiential Worshiper*

From the beginning thought that "Jesus is God's selfie" to the closing image of Dave's dad ripping the black curtain off the altar and shouting "Jesus is risen!" this book can not, should not, and must not be consumed in one sitting. It cries out to be taken morsel by morsel and examined, savored, eaten and digested bit by bit, wit by wit, meme by meme, dream by dream. It is a book that demands time, space, thought, conversation and place. Don't put it on your shelf. Take it into your self. And live with each small piece until it tells you to go on.

—Dr. Rich Melheim
FaithInk.com

Brief, fun and deeply philosophical! This is a power-packed little book that feeds the soul.

—Dr. Tony Ganem
Chief Wellness Officer
BodyPro Fitness Center in Orange County, California
BodyPro.com

Dave Housholder is a man of passion and desire—a passion for Jesus' wisdom and a desire to see all people know the fullness of life in the Spirit. With practical insight he opens to us all that the Creator intends for us to walk in.

—Bishop Steve Wood
Anglican Church in North America.

"Deze man heeft de antwoorden waar jij al je hele leven naar zocht"

In English: "This man has the answers that you've been looking for your whole life long."

—Geert Kimpen,
Best-selling Flemish author of *De Kabbalist*
GeertKimpen.com

David Housholder taps into the joy of God and it pours out as practical wisdom to live the life God dreams for you to live.

—The Rev. Dana Hanson,
Senior pastor, LIFEHouse of Los Angeles
Author of *How to be Christian without being a Jerk*

"Jesus' very life is God's selfie." This apt phrase opens Housholder's book and gives indication of its direction. In short pithy chapters Housholder welcomes readers into an engaging narrative of how to bring the ordinary theology, ordinary faith practices, into meaningful engagement with ordinary life. God is the secret to a meaningful life, and this book welcomes readers into life in God.

—The Rev. Clint Schnekloth,
Author of *Mediating Faith, Faith Formation in a Trans-Media Era*

David Housholder brings hope and joy to the reader with this collection of wisdom artfully interwoven with personal experiences and keen original insights.

—Deaconess Jennifer Clark Tinker
Inspirational Speaker/Writer and Editor-in-Chief
at *Life & Liberty Online Magazine*

"Everyone seeking happiness and meaning in life should read David Housholder's new book *7 Secrets to a Meaningful Life*. David unlocks 7 insights that will help you boldly embrace your God-given strengths."

—Sue Detweiler
Author of *9 Traits of a Life-Giving Mom*
www.SueDetweiler.com

David Housholder's seemingly simple secrets are wrapped in profound complexity; wisdom that only comes from a lifetime of learning and experience. What you will find in *7 Secrets Of A Meaningful Life* are revelations from a very deep well. Not only will you come away having learned something new; but you will be asked to consider the question that may very well forever change your life.

—Mary-Kathryn
Recording Artist
Actress in TV's *Nashville*

ALSO BY THE AUTHOR:

The Blackberry Bush (novel)
blackberrynovel.com

Follow the author on Twitter: @LibertyHous
Author's website: ThornHeart.com

CONTENTS

Chapter One

THE SECRET OF KNOWING GOD

M y wife, Wendy, does not remember the names of all of her grade school teachers. With effort and some research and sleuthing, you could find the names of all of them. You could memorize the classroom numbers and the mailing address of the school. You could even repaint the school from old photos, in watercolors, and display them at a gallery.

In essence, you could escalate your search and find out so much about Wendy that she could not hope to pass a test on herself that you easily would be able to put together.

And you could do this without ever meeting or really knowing Wendy.

We send our kids to Sunday schools, vacation Bible schools, and even set up seminaries with huge libraries full of biblical and theological data. All to teach people facts about God. Nothing wrong with that.

But do you know God?

If not, here's how.

Lay Aside Misconceptions

I remember looking up at the ceiling of a magnificent church in Italy a few years back. There, seated on the throne, was a shirtless, powerful, older man, with a robe across his lap and down to his sandals. His curly white beard and hair framed piercing, serious eyes punctuated by a furrowed brow.

Supposedly, this was God the Father. But he was an exact copy of Zeus, the father-god of ancient Greece.

Where do we get these images of God?

The other common image is that of an invisible Supreme Being. God is an abstract "point of light," impersonal and distant. This higher power is the great Designer, also called the Almighty or Providence.

He gets a nod in the American Declaration of Independence: "endowed by their Creator with certain unalienable Rights . . ." This "Supreme Reason" is really the god of Plato, the god of thoughtful people.

Not that either of these images, the bearded Father on the throne or the invisible First Mover of creation, gets it all totally wrong. But limiting God in any one visual picture or concept leads down the path of sculpting a graven image, which the Bible forbids in the Ten Commandments.

If we have an image of God, we might think we don't need to know the real thing.

Jesus, whose breakthrough wisdom continues to surprise, delight, and challenge us twenty centuries later, gives us another option.

He shocked His followers by saying: "If you had known Me, you would have known My Father also" (John 14:7).

Jesus is God's "selfie."

Rather than a static, fixed, or abstract image, Jesus gifts us with a dynamic and relational picture of the Creator in relationship with us.

Jesus cultivated this I-and-Thou relationship by getting up early and going to secluded places to pray, to line Himself up with the power of God all around Him (Jesus called this the *kingdom*) and to operate in this awareness for the rest of the day.

God is not best found in libraries. He is to be sought daily in our growing awareness of Him, and the actions based on that awareness.

It won't come all at once . . .

> *Little by little, the egg learns to walk.*
> —*Ethiopian Proverb*

. . . so be patient with yourself. It may have taken Jesus thirty years to develop His sense of the Father's presence, power, and work, capped off with a forty-day retreat in the wilderness, before He started His teaching and ministry work.

You will not find God by peering up at paintings on church ceilings. You will not find Him through philosophical inquiry into the tremendous mystery of His supreme direction of the universe.

You will find Him, as Jesus did, early in the morning and throughout the day. Over time your awareness of God will grow, as will your power, joy, and peace.

Jesus' very life is God's selfie.

Soon, people will see the Father's sparkle in the light and life in your eyes—in the selfies you take . . .

And they will ask, "What's different about you lately?"

Application and Discussion

* What are some of the false images of God you may have grown out of over time?

* Are you an impatient person? Do you think this hurts your spiritual development?

* Does it surprise you to think of Jesus as needing time to cultivate His relationship with the Father?

* How is God prompting you with thoughts and questions right now?

* Pay attention to artwork depicting God, Jesus, or spiritual things for the next few weeks. How do they help? How do they get in the way?

Find the Narrow Path

When I go to funerals, it's pretty clear that most people believe nearly everyone goes to heaven; that most people "pass" the course of life. "She's in a better place" floats around the conversations at the lunch after the service.

Hell or spiritual failure is reserved, in the minds of the average citizen, for those who are seriously malicious or evil.

But Jesus says something quite different, even unnerving.

Enter by the narrow gate; for wide is the gate and broad is the way that leads to destruction, and there are many who go in by it. Because narrow is the gate and difficult is the way which leads to life, and there are few who find it.

—Matthew 7:13–14

Granted, Jesus is not specifically talking about heaven and hell here. He is talking about destruction.

Difficult is the way that leads to life, and there are few who find it.

This rings true for me. Indeed, many people do swing and miss at life. As Thoreau penned, "Most men lead lives of quiet desperation."

And Oliver Wendell Holmes left us with:

> *Alas for those that never sing,*
> *but die with all their music in them.*

To round this thought out, Shakespeare's voice echoes down through the centuries:

> *Life's but a walking shadow, a poor player*
> *That struts and frets his hour upon the stage*
> *And then is heard no more: it is a tale*
> *Told by an idiot, full of sound and fury,*
> *Signifying nothing.*[1]

Few find it.

Spiritual failure is all too possible. And it happens all too often.

Your picking up this book shows you have a drive, an *intention* to be one of those few. You seek the narrow gate.

Most people affirm the existence of God. But most people are also barreling down Destruction Highway. Are you ready to upgrade from knowing a few things about God to knowing God in person?

---

1 Shakespeare, William. *Macbeth*, Act 5, Scene 5. Public domain.

Being a large person, I literally have nightmares about narrow doorways and entries. Wriggling through the very goal of life will be a challenge for us all.

We need to exit the eight-lane freeway that leads to destruction, and be willing to follow the path less traveled (as Robert Frost called it).

Jesus did this, and it did not go well for Him. You will end up cutting against the grain of society. You will weather scoldings, exclusion, and social punishment. This may lead to self-doubt and the temptation to merge back onto Destruction Highway.

But Jesus set His face like flint to go to Jerusalem and meet His destiny. I suspect that you will never truly settle for anything less.

Jacob wrestled with an angel until morning and would not let go until the angel blessed him.

Intention, when affirmed day after day, leads to exactly this kind of resolute spirit. A resolute spirit has what it takes to find and enter the narrow entrance.

You will get to know God's heart along the way, and this is what will separate you from those tearing along in the thick traffic of Destruction Highway.

I'll meet you at the narrow gate.

Application and Discussion

* In an era when everyone on the team gets a trophy, is it hard for us to imagine a majority of people failing spiritually in life?

* How do you reconcile God's free gift of grace with Jesus' crystal clear (and jarring) image of the narrow gate?

* What practical things can you decide to do right now to ensure that your intention goes the distance, and that you avoid returning to Destruction Highway?

Start with God's Nature

Let's start with God's nature. Without some wisdom here, we will misread most of the Bible and get stuck on a gerbil wheel of unanswerable questions.

In a nutshell, God is goodness and power.

Compromise this view, and your perception of reality will start to cloud up, like an overcast sky blocking the sun from view.

But clouds do not extinguish the sun.

Shout out "God is good!" in any historically African-American congregation and you will get the visceral response: "All the time!"

Unless you settle this deeply in your heart, the events and circumstances that swirl about the journey of your life will make no sense. Goodness and benevolence are at the core of every square inch of creation. Order. Beauty. Energy. Light.

Anything that is not good is simply not from God.

God cannot give us something He doesn't have: hatred, envy, disease, scarcity, and the like.

All these things are distortions of God's original design. And trying to figure out where all the bad stuff came from will overwhelm your mental capacity and eventually blow your brain's fuse. It's more helpful just to focus on what we can know and what we can do.

And God is *powerful*. But His power is often waiting for us to activate it. Jesus called it the kingdom or God's rule. For whatever reason, God chooses to include us at the boardroom level of His creation. He made us to be partners in His rule—thus the job of "gardeners of the earth" as in the book of Genesis.

It is something for which we are perfectly suited. We are like conduits that carry the power of God into creation.

Your kingdom come.
Your will be done on earth as it is in heaven. (Luke 11:2)

This is the core of the prayer Jesus taught us, commonly known as the Lord's Prayer.

He could direct all of creation Himself, but decided to do something more impressive and beautiful: He shared this rule with us.

When we see something around us that is painful or broken, here is a prayer we should be ready to pray:

Lord, I trust that this brokenness is not from You. There is nothing broken which You cannot fix. Send Your kingdom power through me to help heal this situation now. Your kingdom come, Your will be done on earth as it is in heaven. In Jesus' name, amen.

Unconditional goodness and power waiting for us to use.

Are you ready to be sent into the game? As the Lord scans the earth, He sees that the harvest is great, and the workers are few.

Be one of them. Power awaits.

Application and Discussion

* Does it intimidate you to know that God trusts us to garden the planet?

* How can trying to figure out where evil comes from distract us from joy and power in life?

* Discuss the phrase, "Clouds don't extinguish the sun." What does that mean for our daily lives and trusting God's bright (and hot) goodness?

Know God's Top Priority

Christians from Holland, Switzerland, and Scotland have, for centuries, had a simple answer for the question: What is the meaning of life?

Their young teens had to memorize it.

It was, and still is, listed in the back of their hymnbooks.

Our chief goal is, literally, *to glorify God and to enjoy Him forever.*

Southern Europeans had a different way of saying it; they focused everything on *the love of God.*

Now this phrase can mean two things: our love for God and God's love for us. This back-and-forth action was taught as the main point of human existence.

Note the word *joy* in the midst of *enjoy.*

Love is not a grudging duty. It is given freely or not at all.

But we don't just "fall" into love; we "choose" into love. It is a matter of intention. Doing things on purpose.

And choosing joy is a pretty easy thing. Most of us suffer a joy deficit for days on end.

To enjoy God is to say *yes* to our very being here on this planet. No one asked us if we even wanted to enter the world as a person. Poof! And here we were. We have no memory of anything before our earliest years.

So we get to choose. Granted that since we find ourselves in human form, we can decide to grieve our situation or enjoy it.

My wife's personal quotation in her high school yearbook pronounced that "Things are beautiful if you love them." And if they become beautiful, they are easier to love. Life can cycle up from joy to joy, and from, as the Bible says, glory to glory (2 Cor. 3:18).

But it takes tending the little fire of joy and protecting it. Not letting anyone else or anything—wind, rain, or even neglect—quench it.

This little light of mine, I'm gonna let it shine.

One of the ways we honor and enjoy God is to appreciate each person that crosses our path, for each individual is God's handiwork. His masterpiece.

Sure, we need to have good boundaries, but extending trust to people we meet has been proven good for business and good for our social life. In short, trusting people helps build joy.

When Jesus was asked what are the greatest of the commandments, He answered without missing a beat: to "'love the LORD your God with all your heart, with all your soul, with all your mind, and with all your strength.' This is the first commandment. And the second, like it, is this: 'You shall love your neighbor as yourself'" (Mark 12:30–31).

In short, this intentional effort propels us into a life of joy.

Application and Discussion

* In what ways have you gotten too serious and developed a joy deficit?

* Are you (and others) sometimes hard to motivate because you lack joy?

* How can you cultivate your abilities as a "joy arsonist" among others?

Pursue the Knowledge of God and Stay in God

Knowing God does not always make us comfortable. It does not reinforce our worldviews or sets of pet opinions.

God asserts Himself as quite a character: both in the pages of the Bible and as we engage Him personally in prayer and in life.

God simply refuses to be shoved into a flowchart, and He won't allow you to learn about Him through online classes where you never have to look Him in the face.

God's face shines. One of the oldest blessings recorded by the human race was spoken to Aaron the priest, who in turn spoke to the people of Israel:

> *"The Lord bless you and keep you;*
> *The Lord make His face shine upon you,*
> *And be gracious to you;*
> *The Lord lift up His countenance upon you,*
> *And give you peace."* (Num. 6:24–26)

This is the ultimate. Blessing! ♥

One of the greatest blessings in life is to bask in the presence of the shining face of God.

The Gospel of John features a key word for this unhurried basking: *abiding*. Take the word *staying* and blanket it with heart warmth and receptivity of the soul, and you end up with *abiding*.

One of the most stirring hymns sung in little churches throughout our world ends with:

. . . in life and death O Lord, abide with me . . .

When we abide with the Lord, we are not having a second-hand experience. There is nothing wrong with studying books about God, but as we have mentioned previously, these second-hand encounters can never replace abiding.

Those of us in media-drenched, fast-paced societies have lost our ability to abide, whether with other people or with the Lord.

Our prayers become more and more like fast food when the Lord is setting the table for an all-evening Italian-style meal, lingering with us.

While writing this, I am sitting on the beach in my beloved coastal California. A young family with two toddlers is enjoying life around a fire pit in the sand. The phone is ringing, but I am ignoring it, just drinking in the simple happiness of watching these four people—kids playing and frolicking in the sand, young mom kneeling by the fire, looking up at her husband who proudly tends it. Little Mitchell (they keep calling him to stay close as he toddles off) has just learned to walk and is fascinated by his feet kicking through the sand. Occasionally he hops up and down for pure bliss.

I am blessing the Lord for giving them this evening together as the sun goes down into the pink hues of the horizon to the right of me. I am abiding with the Lord by stopping and paying attention to them. Their joy is my joy.

Abiding means slowing down and enjoying life around us.

Stopping and smelling the flowers. Appreciating color and weather. Knowing what time the sun comes up tomorrow.

You can't stroll with the Lord if you spend your life dashing around in a hurry. Slow down. How was your last breath? Make the next one deeper and slower.

The Bible tells us that the Lord breathed into the clay the breath of life and we became living beings (Gen. 2:7).

There is a place for study. But the Creator of the universe does not call us into the stacks of libraries to find Him.

Little Mitchell has found a stick to poke things with. But with his other hand he reaches out for his kneeling mom. For a moment he abides with her. Certainly her heart is full right now.

The Lord is waiting for you to fill His heart. Abide with Him.

Application and Discussion

* The words *blessing* and *bliss* are closely related. Would it be possible for you to grow in the blessing of others without growing in bliss and joy?

* Blessing others while traveling too fast in life is like shooting arrows from the back of a truck on a bumpy road. Name a few ways we can abide with others so we can better bless them.

* How important is human touch while blessing others? Do you sometimes crave human touch during the day? What can you do to bless others with your physical presence?

Cultivate Presence of Mind

The key to cultivating an ongoing, continuous awareness of God's presence is to do more of what works, and less of what doesn't.

The Lord meets us where we are, and He knows how we are wired. That's why He gives us three aspects of Himself to choose as our own personal entry point to getting to know Him in his fullness: *Father, Son (Jesus), and Holy Spirit.*

The classic teaching of the Christian faith describes God as being fully unified, but having three *persons*—which is just a fancy Latin word for *faces.*

These persons are called God the Father, God the Son (Jesus), and God the Holy Spirit. We humans are all different, and often have preferred entry points for initiating the growth of our relationship with God.

- Those more supernaturally wired often find it's easiest to see God as Spirit. I tend toward this myself. It's easy for me to sense things in the spiritual realm and to trust the existence of realms we cannot see or measure. Transcendent experiences come easy for me, and I am at home in the fiery Christianity of the global south mission fields.

- Those more relationally oriented are often first drawn to Jesus. He is God in a form we can understand and to which we can relate. It's harder to picture walking and talking with the Holy Spirit. I am also deeply drawn to Jesus. I find Him beyond fascinating and would pay almost any price to see what He really looked like and how His temperament came across when he was teaching in New Testament times.

- Those more comfortable with philosophy and mystery like to start with God the Father—beyond our reach and sight, in heaven. They feel right at home with the beginning of the Lord's Prayer. They are, as I am, quick to see the beauty of the Father's design in a flower or a hummingbird. These believers have a heart-level drive to figure out their purpose in the grand design of creation. My friend Joe Johnson often starts his prayers by shouting "Father!"

You see, when you enter into a relationship with God through any of these three doorways, you get all of God because He is not divisible. I am attracted to all three persons of God, but major in the Holy Spirit and minor in Jesus. God the Father, although a positive image for me, does not get my daily walk with Him started in the morning.

For me, breathing in, calming down, and praying "Come, Holy Spirit" (one of the most ancient prayers of the Christian Church) is by far the best way to get things going, and I often end my prayers deep in contemplation about the person of Jesus. The Father and I also have direct contact, but less often.

So be yourself. Start with the person of God that gets your prayer energy humming, then let Him lead you into deeper levels of what He has for you in this very moment.

Mix it up once in a while. Focus on the person of God that is less familiar and see where that takes you.

Whether you are supernaturally, relationally, or philosophically wired, God will start with you exactly where you are.

You come with all the software you need for a living, full, and satisfying relationship with your Maker.

It's time to enjoy Him forever. Start today.

Application and Discussion

* Which of the three persons of God has the biggest pull on you?

* Are you more supernaturally, relationally, or philosophically wired?

* How does a spiritual practice based on your basic temperament look on a day-to-day basis? How can it be cultivated?

Avoid the Gutters

We can't cultivate abiding in God's presence if we don't look at the "root twin" of that word: *present.*

Nothing exists in the past or the future. I hate to disappoint you science-fiction time-travel fans, but you can't go to a time that is just an illusion. You could achieve Bill Gates' wealth, and make use of all the technology that will ever be developed, and yet time travel will remain a mirage.

You see, images in our minds can seem very real. We've all awakened from dreams that terrified us with their picture-perfect imitations of life. Memories work much the same way—especially those with powerful emotional content.

We can wax nostalgic the minute an old song wafts through the drugstore while we are shopping. The memories attached to that song wash over us like a wave. But the events in our memory simply aren't happening—anywhere. They no longer exist.

Same with the future. Those of us who navigate extensive to-do lists and work on complex projects can project our hearts into a future that is no less a chimera than the past. It ain't there either. Nowhere to be found.

The future can conjure up all kinds of worry. The past can produce all kinds of regret and shame.

But neither have anything to do with reality. That takes place only in the here and now.

And in the here and now, we can only take one step at a time. Complete one action at a time.

A proverb common to many cultures goes something like this:

> *A present well-lived leads to an upgraded tomorrow*
> *and rich memories in your past.*

Being able to shut out the gutter balls of dwelling on the past and/or future is the secret to keeping the bowling ball of life in the lane and hitting a few pins.

Most unhappy people I know have a tiny future that is overwhelmed by their past, where their heart truly lives. They're fretting about the future tears layers from their stomach linings. They can't stay in the present.

The same is true with your prayer practice. If you are always bargaining with God—dwelling on sins you've committed (past) or asking Him to do all kinds of things (future) for you—then it's no wonder that you are having a hard time sensing His presence (there's that word again!).

If you were the Creator of the universe, wouldn't you be more interested in what people were doing right now than with what they did last Thursday? Or next Wednesday?

Most happy people love hanging out in the here and now. They are able to love others and enjoy the little things in life. They aren't rushing off to meet some future deadline. And, surprisingly, they tend to do better work and often get paid more because they have developed the ability to pay attention to what they are doing. Olympic gold medalists have a vise-like grip on the present. As do top salespeople.

There are many ways to get better at living in the here and now. One is by paying attention to your breathing. Isn't that what your mom told you to do when you got all worked up? How was your last breath? Slow the next one down. Learn to listen. I'm listening to a jet fly by. There's a slight hum of cars behind me. A group of young adults in the park ahead of me is engaged in spirited flirting with a lot of punch and joy in their voices. Two teen boys are playing catch with a football, and I hear a gentle *slap* each time it is caught. A young, husky boy just shuffled by, scraping his flip-flops on the sandy pavement and dragging the corner his boogie board on the ground behind him. The light, machine-like ratchet click of two spinning bike wheels just whizzed past. A car door just slammed shut.

Take a moment to listen. Paying attention is the key to finding peace and being productive.

Guard against the gutter balls of past and future dwelling.

Life is a gift; that's why we call it the present.

Application and Discussion

* It has been said that as soon as your past is bigger than your present and future, you become old. What do you think of that?

* Does your to-do list get so big and long that you end up living way into the future, unable to appreciate the here and now?

* Think of a joyful person you know who lives in the present. What would keep you from being more like him or her?

* What success have you had in cultivating good habits of any kind? How can you apply these techniques to cultivating a temperament of joy?

Chapter Two

THE SECRET OF KNOWING YOURSELF

Accurate self-knowledge, gained objectively by valuable input from long-term relationships, is the royal road to personal effectiveness. Like any good investment, self-knowledge produces compounding benefits. It takes a while, so start today. Here's how . . .

Grow in Self-Awareness

Have you ever sat in a circle at a twelve-step recovery or rehab group?

It can be a spiritually electric environment, yet rather pedestrian and unimpressive at the same time. Not really flashy, but they know how to push life's big gears.

One little verse weaves its way through all such groups; Niebuhr's matchless Serenity Prayer: "God grant me the serenity to accept the things I cannot change, courage to change the things I can, and wisdom to know the difference."

We can change far more things about ourselves than we believe. Experts tell us that the mind is much more elastic than we ever previously believed. Almost any of our thoughts, behaviors, and habits can be redirected and upgraded.

But the Bible also tells us that we cannot even change the color of one hair on our heads. And there are other limitations on our transformation:

- Getting taller once we have reached adulthood
- Changing our past and our history
- Changing our eye color or right/left handedness
- Avoiding the need for reading glasses as we age
- Making our hair go curly if it is straight

I'm sure you can think of a few more if you put your mind to it.

You were also hardwired, born with abilities and talents. There are simply some things that drive others crazy with difficulty, but which come easily to you.

I'm especially good at fixing mechanical devices (engines, etc.) that are unfamiliar to me, and also at deciphering things—even dead languages. But on the other hand, I have no timeline "app" in my head, and calendars are an absolute nightmare to me. I live under the constant dread that I am missing something important or failing to keep a promise because I don't know what's coming next without looking it up.

So knowing ourselves amounts to one big lived-out Serenity Prayer. Our task is to maximize our talents and to minimize the effects (on us and on others) of our downsides.

My mentor, Pastor Maynard Nelson, once confided to me: "We all have our own ladders into hell (natural propensity toward brokenness). We need to know where they are and learn to stay far away from them."

But dwelling on little flaws is a waste of time. As long as you protect yourself from the effects of your biggest flaws, it's better to focus on your strengths. For it is there, and not in overcoming petty weaknesses, that you will find the secret of what you can contribute to creation.

The Greeks considered it one of the highest virtues to "Know thyself." This book is a power-tool helping you to do exactly that.

Application and Discussion

* We often think we know ourselves better than we actually do. What keeps us from self-awareness? What can we do to get a more objective look at ourselves?

* What are some of your inborn talents? What comes easily to you?

* What are your ladders into hell? Your weak spots? Your vulnerabilities? How do you keep your distance from them?

Humble Yourself

I'd like to put a warning sign on the road to humility that would scream "Danger Ahead!"

Misguided teaching on humbleness (humility) has done more to damage the self-esteem of weaker people and keep them from empowerment and happiness than anything I know.

When misused, humility can cause codependency and a doormat mentality, which does nothing but feed the ambition of predatory people who know where to find easy prey and can smell your low self-worth in a New York minute.

Another place where the devil loves to distort the concept of humility is your prayer life. I once heard a woman say, "The Lord must have given me stomach cancer to humble me and make me more dependent on Him." Yikes. What kind of cosmic abuser would do such a thing? What kind of father would do that to a child?

False humility is also used to "ego-ize" in religious settings. Praying out loud in public for "more personal humbleness" is a way of signaling your conceit and superiority to others. I often see this in Christian athletic circles.

So what is true humility? Once again, let's look at God's "selfie"—Jesus. This man from Nazareth was anything but unassertive. Yet He knew His place. Subservient toward God the Father; totally one of us in the flesh; honoring those around Him; and teaching us to "love others as we love ourselves" and to "do unto others . . ."

Humility for you and me means to follow Jesus' example, putting ourselves under God and totally on the same level with everyone else (even enemies). You can't say:

> *No one is better or more important than me . . .*

without its corollary:

> *I am no better or valuable than anyone else.*

But our competitive society continues to rank us by grade point average, net worth, popularity, Klout Score, etc. Wanting to be special (more valuable than others) is a head trip. We are brainwashed into valuing competitive rankings, constantly terrified that we are going to lose points on the big public scoreboard.

One who believes in biblical humility rejects this ratings game and speaks in unison with Thomas Jefferson, who so eloquently penned: "We hold these truths to be self-evident, that all men are created equal."

That, my friend, is true humility.

Application and Discussion

∗ Have you ever struggled with self-esteem problems? Where did they come from? Competitive society? False "humility" teaching which you embraced? Has your broken self-esteem been made worse by the hymns or sermons of the church?

∗ Competition can be fun and productive. Singing contests on TV. Seasons of *The Bachelor*. The Olympics. The market-place. But what are the mortal dangers of connecting and ranking our self-esteem by our scores?

∗ Be honest. Whom do you look down upon? What kind of person elicits a proud or hateful thought from you?

∗ Pray for the next five strangers to cross your path. Ask the Lord to show you how you and each person are equal in His eyes . What surprises you about this exercise?

Throttle Your Thoughts

Imagine you are driving to work on a freeway.

Familiar landmarks on your daily route whiz by. The muscle memory in your arms makes each twist and turn with well-worn, autopilot familiarity. The gut feeling, which accompanied your awakening from slumber, carried with it the still present orphaned emotional fragments of dreams, the story line of which vanished with the sound of your alarm clock.

Free of facing any real challenges as you drive, your mind begins to run wild. Like a slide show of random impulses, thoughts make their way one at a time onto your main screen.

The emotional soundtrack is a mix of feelings that you don't question—it just colors the mood of the "show" of serial thoughts.

Many of us never notice that we have access to the remote that controls the slide show. We don't have to be passive victims of its scene selection. We can pause, erase, search, or even reverse what shows on the screens of our conscious minds.

Those who are aware of their remote and use it have what we call a disciplined mind. They choose their thoughts; their thoughts don't choose them.

What we often diagnose as ADD or ADHD is in many cases simply an undisciplined mind. Those who work unsupervised at home or on the road can waste a lot of precious time engaged in this random kaleidoscope of thoughts. This is why many of us watch TV—so that the ceaseless waterfall of images stops and takes on some orderliness as our internal slide show conforms to program. It "takes our minds off" of our all-too-often bewildering and exhausting existences.

The Bible calls us to take "every thought into captivity" (2 Cor. 10:5). In other words, to think intentionally and to choose our mental slide show—perhaps even picking out the emotional soundtrack. Those who have learned to do this have almost unlimited social and spiritual power. They know that thoughts create words, and words (especially those spoken aloud in faith) can create reality.

In this sense, we humans are reality-generating machines, made in the very image of God. The book of Hebrews calls this bringing forth that which is not (yet) by faith.

So how do we let go of thoughts that come randomly, so that we can think thoughts that are intentional (and thus powerful), in their place? What I use is this simple phrase:

If thoughts can come, thoughts can go.

And rather than chase the unwanted images out of my mind, I simply pay them no attention and let them slip away on their own. Then I decide for myself what I am going to think about. I try not to get frustrated with myself—sometimes I have to "let go and get going" several times before intentional thought kicks in.

As Martin Luther said about five hundred years ago: you can't keep a bird from flying over your head, but you can keep it from building a nest in your hair.

This has obvious applications for prayer. Whether prayer is more thought-and-conversation based (what Paul called praying with the mind) or more akin to spiritual communion (what he called praying with the spirit), it always benefits from an uncluttered, disciplined mind.

Start practicing taking your thoughts captive today. Let random thoughts slide right past you, and replace them with thoughts you choose . . . on purpose.

Application and Discussion

* Why do you suppose no one ever teaches us how to keep our thoughts intentional while praying?

* Many people give up on prayer because their minds wander. Does this happen to you?

* Do you think it's possible to go a whole day without consciously choosing your thoughts? Do you ever go to bed at night thinking, "Where did this day go?"

* Practice letting uninvited thoughts go. Let them slide on by. A focused mind is a power-tool. What time of the day would be best for you to practice this skill?

Understand Your Emotions

Much the same can be said of thoughts and emotions.

Come with me, if you will, to a vegetable garden. I was in charge of ours when I was a young teen, and I spent many happy hours there in the spring, summer, and fall. The radishes were always the first to come up. One of them always had some kind of bug or worm eating it up—a vivid memory.

By the end of the summer, my corn, much taller than I was, ripened and beckoned to be picked. From one little kernel had grown this majestic plant full of what would become hot, buttered, sweet corn.

The key to gardening is intentionality, planting, and cultivation. The same is true with your emotions. An undisciplined heart will reflect, just like a chameleon, the feelings of those people around you.

The Bible says we reap what we sow. So the key for me is to plant seeds of:

- Joy
- Peace and Tranquility
- Contentment
- Patience
- Graciousness
- Alertness

You can choose your own list of feelings toward which to take aim.

It's important for me to write down how I want to feel at the end of the day, not just what I want to get done. If I don't plant a garden with intention, all I will get is a weed patch.

So often that's what our emotional matrix looks like—head-high briars and thick with dandelions and weeds. Well, we reap what we sow.

At the end of the day, I want to feel joy, shalom, and a sense of forward momentum. I set my intentions in the morning and try to get there over the arc of the day.

Does the day always turn out perfectly? Of course not. But when I do this, it turns out way better than when I am not intentional about it.

The year 2013 was a very rough one for me, emotionally speaking. Blow after blow came in like crashing waves at the shore, the kinds that knock you over and roll you around when you try to stand up to them.

Then 2014 came around, and I could have just continued that pattern. A few misfortunes piled up, but I decided that I was going to feel good about 2014, every evening, no matter what the circumstances. I chose to have a good year.

Did I always succeed? No. I sometimes went to bed frustrated and alienated at the end of the day.

Was my emotional state still many times better than 2013, even though the circumstances were not all that different at first? Absolutely.

I had learned the skill of emotional intentionality.

But gardening also takes cultivation, not just sowing seed. The more attention we give to our cash crops, the more they thrive.

Weeding out the negative, reactive emotions is one of the skills we must master if we are to garden our emotions.

This allows more sunlight to shine on our positive states of being, described well as the fruit of the Spirit in Galatians 5:22–23: "love, joy, peace, longsuffering, kindness, goodness, faithfulness, gentleness, self-control."

Along with weeding, we need to reward ourselves for thinking good thoughts. The Bible calls us to focus on whatever is beautiful and true. Give yourself an attaboy/attagirl when you react to something, anything, with peace and depth of joy.

Seeding and cultivation. Be intentional and let your emotional garden grow . . . with joy.

Application and Discussion

* What do you think about this statement: "It is better to choose your emotions than to let them choose themselves"?

* Can we be seen as uncompassionate if we don't affirm someone's negativity when they are in a dark place? What's a wise way to handle this?

* Why is solid joy (not just yippie-skippie stuff) a good place to aim? What are some other good emotional targets? Make a list.

* What happens when we water weeds in a real garden? What happens when we dwell on negative thoughts in our emotional garden?

Listen to Your Body

As you read this, pay attention to what your body is saying. How does your gut feel after what you just read? Is your heart settled or restless? Is there some hunger or thirst trying to make itself known?

The truth is, your consciousness and awareness do not take place in your brain alone. We feel and experience life with our whole selves—our whole bodies.

The writers of the Bible has a vitalized world view. The Greek writers of the New Testament saw *zoë* or *life force* as an intangible but recognizable quality. It's easy for a ten-year-old to see when something's dead and lacking life-stuff. This *élan vital*, as the French call it, drives empirical scientists nuts, because they can't measure or quantify it. Though they often try to deny its existence, you and I, and almost everyone, intuit that zoë is there. We operate accordingly. We even call the study of animals *zoology* and take our kids to visit the *zoo*. These words are grandkids of this biblical root concept.

Paul says that this same power that raised Jesus from the dead lives in all of us.

Feeling alive is not just an on-or-off switch. Like a nice lamp, it can be turned up. Wouldn't you like to increase the percentage of each day where you feel fully alive? Wouldn't this have a big influence on your physical health and your relationships?

Zoë doesn't just occur in our brains; it inhabits every living cell in our bodies. This quality exudes preciousness and value, and we sense it in our gut when we feel certain things. We can tell if our hearts are settled or restless with life, and perhaps we even feel zoë in our fingertips when we notice the nearby presence of the Holy Spirit.

Breath feeds this life force, and the Bible tells us how God breathes into inert matter this breath of life to create living beings. In both the major original languages of the Bible, Hebrew and Greek, the ancients used the same word, not separate labels, for *spirit* and *breath*. To them, they were more or less the same thing.

Modern thinking has cheapened this rich (and more accurate) view of life. We are taught nowadays that 100 percent of the action happens in our brains, which are really just complex computers, and that are bodies are just machines that more or less make sure our brains make it to meetings.

How sad that we have flattened and denaturalized our description of the glory of human existence and awareness.

The biblical view of humankind is so much more sophisticated, nuanced, and explanatory than today's mechanical view. For instance, your heart is so much more than a pump. It is the core of your existence.

And what do we check as vital signs if we find someone crumpled on the ground? Breath. And heartbeat. Signs of zoë life.

Cultivate this life in yourself and help others to burn brighter. We see those around us whose lamps are flickering. Fan them into flame with encouragement and prayer.

Burn hot. Burn bright. Burn with life.

Application and Discussion

* When you get sick, do you naturally see your body as a simple machine that needs chemicals (drugs) to fix it, or do you see it as this and so much more?

* Why do you think some nonbelieving scientists dismiss the idea of soul, spirit, or zoë when it has been so obvious to so many people for so many millennia that we are more than the sum of our parts?

* How bright, on a scale of one to ten, is your flame of life burning today? How can you brighten yourself this week?

* Has encouragement from someone else ever turned your flame up? Remember that when you encourage others!

Maximize Your Strengths

Soar with your strengths.

We notice our shortcomings, emotionally speaking, more than we see our own strengths.

Beauty has been defined as the greatest action accomplished with the most ease. This is why we need others to notice, identify, and inform us of our strengths. We tend to see them as effortless, and somehow believe that everyone has the same abilities we do.

Our gifted areas tend to hang out in our blind spots. Others see them but we usually don't.

However, we are painfully aware of our flaws and shortcomings. We dwell on them, wasting precious emotional energy that should be spent pushing the big gears of our strengths.

Think about your last job review. Doing some deep breathing before going into your boss's office, you calmed yourself and tried not to look at the "growth areas" section of your evaluation—even though your boss was trying to look you in the eye and to thank you for your solid accomplishments during the year.

The phrase "needs to work on" sent a sting through your system, and you started to feel very vulnerable and unsafe.

You walked back to your desk, convinced your boss saw right through you and that you would get fired. Fight-or-flight reflexes may even have kicked in. The next day, when you'd calmed down, you noticed that your review was 80% positive.

The more you live in true community, however, the more others will notice your gifts. You will begin to see a pattern in their comments about you and start to adjust your vocation and life around those things.

The more isolated you are, however, the more socially unattractive you will feel as you fixate on your flaws. This is one of the reasons loners end up depressed.

In order to soar with your strengths, the biggest key is to invest in go-the-distance, nonnegotiable relationships. These are the people who were put in place to bring out the very best "you" that will ever walk this earth.

And you get to bless them by noticing their gifts. What a deal!

Application and Discussion

* Were you taught, growing up, that noticing your own gifts was boastful? How can you grow in awareness of your strengths without making others feel bad by comparison?

* Are you afraid to appear in a swimsuit in the summer on the beach? What is it about our flaws that control our behaviors? Why does one red pimple on our face get all of our attention? Does media reinforce our tendency to fixate on and hide our flaws?

* What would happen to the direction of your life if you prayed, out loud, every day, "Lord, show me my strengths and help me soar with them today to Your glory"?

* Imagine a day where you put more emotional energy into your strengths than into worrying about your flaws. Now imagine a week. A month. A year. You get the idea . . .

* How can you prepare for your next job review with your boss in such a way that you won't over-focus on the negative?

Be Bold

I just left my laptop in my van and went out and fed the seagulls with a box of stale crackers that I had neglected.

It was fascinating to watch. There were fast gulls and aggressive gulls. They were followed by tentative gulls and birds lacking awareness.

Every time I threw a cracker onto the sun-drenched wet sand along the wave action of the water, the fast birds would swoop in and swoop out. Next came the aggressive birds who would posture and peck at each other (finding the fight more important than actually getting the cracker). The tentative gulls watched from a distance, wishing they had the courage to take part. And the rest were sleeping or oblivious . . .

The obvious winners were the bold, fast birds, who were long gone with their crackers just seconds before the fighting birds started up with their loud-squawking sumo-stuff. These pro-wrestler gulls were often still fighting minutes after the crackers were all eaten up. The scared birds are most likely still regretting not giving it a shot, and the sleepy birds hardly even wonder what happened.

Jesus was one of the fast birds. He got more done in three years (in terms of His impact on the world) than any other human got done in a lifetime. Sure, it's riskier. It got Him killed in the end. But He was in and out like lightning, on His way to the next town before the fighting birds (Pharisees and scribes) could inflict much damage.

There's a great image of Him in the Bible walking into a synagogue and saying outrageous things. Arguments started and the rabble ended up trying to bring Him up to a cliff to throw Him off. (I have seen that cliff in Nazareth, and it's not for the faint of heart or the acrophobic.) He slipped through their fingers like wet soap and was on to His next assignment before they knew what had happened.

The Romans had a saying: "Fortune Favors the Brave." There was no analysis paralysis in Jesus' thinking, for He was a man of decisive action. Setting the agenda Himself, He went through every door the Father left ajar for Him.

This took keen alertness on His part, which was honed to razor-sharp clarity with hours of prayer—off by Himself as was His custom, dialing in to what the Father was doing in His creation that day. Hardly one of the sleepy birds.

The Bible even encourages us to do the same, to go "boldly to the throne of grace" and get what we need (Heb. 4:16). The woman with the issue of blood was bold and decisive: "If only I may touch His garment, I shall be made well" (Matt. 9:21). No endless "begging wishing" prayers. She slashed through the crowd and got it done. Didn't even ask first. Just took her healing.

The Lord is opening all kinds of doors for you today. Which kind of seagull are you going to be? Swift, fighting, timid, or clueless?

You have what it takes. The Bible says you have the mind of Christ. It says the Holy Spirit will teach you all things. It claims you won't have to worry about what to say—but that God will give you the words. God looks back and forth across the earth, looking for some fast birds open to some tremendous opportunities.

Why not be one of those people?

Carpe diem. Seize the day. It's the Jesus way of being.

Application and Discussion

* My grandfather gave me great advice: "When you walk into a room, act like you belong there." How can we get better at that?

* When making a suggestion in a group, are you afraid people won't value it, or do you assume that they will? Do you expect people to laugh at your jokes?

* Decisive action risks failure. And the truth is, take all the wildly successful people you know, and failure is the least of their fears. They welcome it as a chance to learn and upgrade themselves. What do you think holds people back most: external factors, luck, or their own risk-aversion?

* Rick Warren once said, in a lecture I heard in person, "If you are going to fail, fail quickly!" As you age, are you more or less the victim of "analysis paralysis"? Why?

* Do others see you as one of the fast birds? How can you start to change their opinion of you?

Chapter Three

THE SECRET OF LOVE

The multiuse word *love* covers vast mileage on the waterfronts of our souls. We use it for specialized things, like describing the essence of romance or marriage. But it doesn't have to refer to our connections to other humans—we can also love sunsets and cheeseburgers. And I happen to feel pretty strongly about both of them!

Love can refer to deep feelings of emotional loyalty toward our homeland or reverence for the beauty of nature. Both often bring tears to my eyes, and perhaps yours too.

But for the next few pages we are going to exclude much of that and focus on love between you and other beings—humans and your Creator:

- Courtship and marriage
- Family relationships
- Friendships
- Colleagues

How's that going for you? Would you like to have more of this thing called relational love? Or has it eluded your grip for most of your life?

Experience Love, Give Love

Picture yourself as a big goblet outside in a warm rainstorm. The spattering drops are drenching everything and filling the cup, which sloshes and overflows at a certain point, soaking the already soggy wood of the picnic table.

This is a perfect illustration of how love works.

The warm rainwater represents love. You are the goblet. The bigger the capacity of the goblet, the more love you can hold.

Perhaps you've heard the Bible story of the widow and the miracle of the oil jars. A great wonder occurred, and the oil jars started filling up. She ran around begging and borrowing more containers—which also filled spontaneously with oil. At last she could find no more jars. And the oil stopped flowing.

God doesn't run out of oil (or warm water of love). We run out of capacity to receive it. King David says in the twenty-third Psalm: "My cup runs over."

We don't have to beg the Creator to send us love. His capacity is boundless, and He has more than enough for everyone. God simply scans the earth looking for those with the will and capacity to receive.

God's love comes to us free from above. We do nothing to earn it. But we often lack the intention to take as much of it as we can get. We sit indoors with a thimble of a cup and wonder why we feel so thirsty for living water.

And why do we want more? Out of some strange spiritual gluttony or greediness? By no means. It is so we can have enough for gallons of this godly love we've received to spill over the sides and onto others.

We don't please God by avoiding mistakes and petty sins as much as we please Him with our willingness to receive—for the sake of others. Receiving not just love, but abundance, resources, wisdom, health, healing, and everything our world needs more of. And, the side effect of receiving so much from Him that it pours over the sides? We are less prone to sin and mistakes!

You see, God lives to give. He is the Lord and giver of life. And when we ask for more than we need (abundance) we have more to share.

Do you struggle with the sense that God is distant? That He talks to everyone but you? Wanna know a secret about how to close that distance? Simple: receive so much that you become a joyful giver of life and love to others. Guess what will happen? You will be lining up with the downward-giving vector of God. And when you're lined up with Him, you'll feel close to Him. You will be in a deep partnership with the life and love that He pumps into creation on a constant basis.

We want more love from God, not so we can hoard it, but so we can let it flow though us—becoming part of His rainstorm, which nourishes creation.

So cultivate daily time where you can soak in the Lord's presence. At first it may feel selfish, awkward, and indulgent. But remember what they say on airplanes: "First affix your own oxygen mask and then assist others."

Watch your body language while you practice this prayer of receiving. Open hands, face turned slightly upward, heart open, shoulders back. And the prayer can be so simple: "More, Lord. More of You. Increase my capacity to receive from You." Breathe deep. You are a lot bigger on the inside than you are on the outside, and the Lord has more love for you than you can ever hope to receive. The Apostle Paul describes this in Ephesians 3. Describing for us his soaking sessions, he tells us that the Love of God is so broad, deep, and wide that we will never be able to experience all of it.

We were put here to nurture God's creation. And God brought this very creation forth—especially this lush, green planet—to nurture us.

So loving others is just letting God's love, gifts, and resources flow through you to them. And the greatest joy? When you teach others to have their own life-giving relationships directly with God and they, like you, become givers of the boundless resources of God.

Application and Discussion

* What do you think of the phrase: "I don't need much to get by"?

* What keeps you from soaking in God's presence?

* In what specific ways do we receive more from God's creation when we invest more in nurturing others? Is nurturing going both ways (between you and creation) or is it out of balance? What steps can you take to get it into balance?

Go the Distance

I grew up in a wonderful family, but we now span three of the four American time zones. We moved a lot when I was growing up, and I learned to dispose of and make new friendships quickly. I'm much like a military kid; you'll think I'm your friend after talking to me for an hour.

My two brothers, a couple of my favorite people on earth, and I studied in different places, met and married wives from two different states and a foreign country, and live at the points of a triangle that has four to five thousand miles to its three sides. In my profession, I was trained to stay about five years on the job, and then to move on—hopefully to a "promotion" of sorts.

My life has been a true joy, and I'm grateful for the wisdom that comes from living in many places and having good interactions with so many kinds of people. But there is a downside. Most of my relationships have been functionally disposable. I wasn't really going the distance with anyone except my wife and son. Sure, I was still cordial with those from previous seasons of life, but we weren't "doing life together" anymore. We just did Christmas cards, and in later years, Facebook.

In my forties I grew profoundly dissatisfied with this, and my wife and I became intentional about "permanentizing" our friendships with three other couples in our Bible and prayer group. My wife is investing in her girlfriends, and I am spending more time with the guys I surf with.

Tonight as I write this, we are planning the funeral for the mother of Lou from our couples' group; and I just got a text from Bruce to meet him for surfing tomorrow morning at 7:15 a.m. We've been friends with this batch of people for going on twelve years now, and we fully intend, as much as it's in our power, to go the distance with all of them.

You see, our relationships have become more important than whatever problems we could or will have with these friends. More important than new jobs or promotions that would cause us to dispose of life together with them.

We are members of a wonderful, funky little church. It is the ninth church Wendy and I have joined since marrying thirty-two years ago. But we have been with these people for twelve years, and there is nothing that could happen at this church that could cause us to "look for another church where we would be better fed." People break fellowship with churches all the time and look elsewhere. Why? Their problems are bigger than their relationships.

What if you turned that on its head? What would happen to marriages, work partnerships, customer-business relationships, and plain old fun relationships if we put loving people ahead of our problems with them personally?

You see, we are eternal beings; and if we can't figure out how to treat the important people in our lives as nondisposables for these fleeting decades, how can we hope to have fellowship forever in the heavenlies?

If you go the distance with people, your love for them will grow because you will stop trying to find fault with them (a subconscious way of keeping score so we can justify tossing them out at some point). We will stop avoiding conflict because we know that we will have to deal with our friends and family at some point. We can't just walk away.

God promises: "I will never leave you nor forsake you" (Heb. 13:5). It's when we line up like Him with others that we start to bask in the light of God's love, getting an inkling of how He feels about us.

Our loyalty doesn't have to be toward everyone. Even Jesus focused on and went deep with Peter, James, and John, and to a lesser extent, the rest of the twelve and the key women.

My grandfather once told me when I was in college: "If you have six men to carry your casket to that hole in the ground, men that really care about you and know what's going on in your life, nothing else in life will compare to that success. Most of us are lucky to die with two or three of them."

Who's got your back for the duration? Having friends like these will cost you a lifetime of loyalty—but it will be so very worth it. As the Bible says, love endures all things and bears all things. Life is hard. Who are your faithful compadres and comadres?

Application and Discussion

* Name three go-the-distance people in your life. Do they know you feel that way about them? What conversations need to take place for them to know about your commitment to them?

* Were you more committed to a handful of people when you were younger, or is that loyalty growing stronger now? What can you do this week to keep things moving in a good direction?

* What do you think of the question: "Are your relationships bigger than your problems?"

Be Present

As I was writing (which I love to do outdoors) the previous segment of this book just five minutes ago, a six-foot-tall, typical California beach girl came rollerblading up to my VW bus here on the bike path along the beach. My mother-in-law from

Europe calls such women "American corn-fed beauties." But she was lacking the typical sunshine smile that comes from living in great weather with lots of extraverted people for one's whole life.

Her voice was shaky, and I heard some desperation in her tone when she tentatively asked: "I just hate to bother you, but do you have an Allen wrench?" I replied from my beach chair outside the bus, looking up from my laptop, "Sure."

I had just enjoyed some wonderful soaking-prayer time earlier in the afternoon, and I was feeling very "together"—productive and relaxed, despite lots of deadlines and promises to keep.

But back to the story at hand. Of course I have an Allen wrench. Two kinds, both with all the different sizes lined up in order. I am the consummate tool nerd; have been ever since I was a little kid. The prized possession I would grab if my house were on fire is a pair of light-blue gripped Craftsman channel-lock pliers I've had since seventh grade. She showed me the wheel that was wobbling—and I noticed that her left leg was still shivering from trying to force this wayward skate to stay in balance, perhaps for miles. I tried tightening the wheel but it didn't help. The threads seemed stuck or stripped.

So I asked her to lean against the outside of my bus so I could take my time and fix it correctly. I removed the axle and reset it correctly. Then I retightened it from the outside. I noticed the quality craftsmanship of these expensive skates—she had likely just made the problem worse by trying to adjust it, and had put the screw back in wrong.

I made it very clear to her that I had plenty of time to do this right. She was so very grateful, testing it out before skating away. "You saved me a three-mile walk without shoes."

California bustles along at a busy, if not frenetic, pace. People can count on one hand the moments when others take the time with them to attend to their needs, asking nothing in return.

My calm and lack of hurry changed the very tone of her voice as I explained what I was doing to her axle and wheel. As she departed with a friendly wave on a smoothly gliding skate, I reminded her to "enjoy that sunset in about twenty minutes, and stay warm as it gets cooler this evening." She probably didn't even hear it since she had her iPhone earbuds in . . .

Did I have time to do that? No. I'm still behind. But putting people in front of tasks is a great rule for life. I could have easily fibbed—no one expects you to have an Allen wrench with you when you're typing on a laptop, seated on a bike path.

I gave her a little time and help—signs of God's love. And you know what? I felt more full of God's love after giving aid than before she skated up in the first place.

In fact, I'm certain that the Lord prompted her, whether she sensed the source of the prompting or not, to come to me, knowing that I'm probably the only one nearby with the correct tools.

Love is not a zero-sum game. The more you give, the more it grows inside of you so you can give even more to others next time. You don't end up lacking in love because you give it.

And the key to being present with people is slowing down, having intentions for your interaction, not trying to control the outcome (a tricky balance), and remembering that God values both of you equally.

Another thing that helps me? I avoid worrying about what anyone thinks of me while interacting with them. We have no access to people's thoughts, let alone any control over what they think of us. And it's just plain distracting to go there. It's hard enough to pay attention to your own thoughts and to observe the actions and words of others. Worrying about their opinions of you is unhelpful at best and self-deceiving at worst. Just be yourself. It will be good enough.

Application and Discussion

* In what way do interruptions bother you? What would change if you started to see some of them as opportunities?

* If you feel uncomfortable when alone with people, what do you suppose causes this? What kinds of things can you do to learn to be more comfortable in the presence of others?

* Can you have a one-on-one conversation with someone, look her in the eye, and be okay with not saying anything to "fill the silence?" Try practicing it this week.

* In what ways can task-orientation get in the way of people-orientation?

* Tell a story about how a random encounter changed your life. What would have happened if you had ignored the interruption?

Listen Better, Communicate Better

Dr. Randy Jacobs, after examining me for what appeared to be exhaustion and pneumonia, sat down on one of those round stools with wheels in his exam room in the small town of Port Townsend, Washington.

I was a young pastor just a couple of years out of school, married with a young son. I was trying to prove myself. And my usually strong body was giving out.

Realizing the cause of the problem, Randy sat down and looked at me. His body language was very clear. Despite a waiting room full of people, he had all the time in the world.

"So, tell me. What's really going on?"

The next moment froze in my mind. Time stood still, and I said to myself, "He's really going to listen." I couldn't remember the last time someone had done that. For the next twenty-five minutes or so, I gave him the whole story. Not a word from him. No *uh-huhs*. Nothing. But his eyes said, "Go on. I'm listening."

"You need time off." He pulled out his prescription pad and wrote: "One week at the lodge in Lake Quinault. I'll pay for it."

He told me to get my family and leave right away for the several-hour drive. He'd ensure that my work duties were covered by people in my field whom he knew well. I was on my way to Lake Quinault with Wendy and Lars within the hour.

If this happens to you a handful of times in your life, you are average. The truth is, we don't listen much or get listened to much. We talk *at* each other. We formulate answers before the other person is finished talking. We tell long boring stories without checking in to see if anyone is even listening. Some of us fall in love with the sound of our own voices. But the sad thing is, those around us have more talk than we have listen.

And when we really need a listening ear, it's hard to find.

The greatest compliment that was ever paid me was when
one asked me what I thought, and attended to my answer.
—Henry David Thoreau[2]

Loving is enhanced by listening. Listening bonds people and allows love to flow more freely between them.

Good listeners stop what they are doing and show that they are stopping. In this case, a busy doctor took his seat and looked at me. If we barrel along through our days without pausing, we will never cultivate the staple food of love—listening.

Good listeners give up control of the conversation and stop guessing where it is going to go. Dr. Jacobs was obviously befuddled that a young, strong man would be so sick. Being one of the smartest men in town, he may have been tempted to hurry in with a guess; but he resisted and was truly open to hearing from me so he could learn more.

After breaking the endless chain of busyness and giving up control of the outcome, good listeners then tune out the rest of the world and put their full attention to listening. A cultivated prayer life helps build muscles for this. Receptivity, toward God or others, is receptivity. A healthy prayer life thus makes us better listeners.

The last step is to speak your best wisdom into the situation, only after the other person is truly finished, with love and a true will to do everything you can to help the other person. Ask the Lord to give you the resources and insight to make a real and lasting difference as you speak. God brought that other person (the speaker) to you (the listener) because you are the one most

---

2 Thoreau, Henry David. Essay: "Life Without Principle." Public domain.

able to help. Dr. Jacobs, one of the most prosperous and influential people in town, was the only one who could have given me the answer he did and make it stick. And the resting made me well.

Remember what your mom said when teaching you to cross the street? Same goes for listening:

Stop. Step out of your momentum-filled, box-checking, task-oriented rush.

Look. Look at the person before you. Look at yourself and guard against coming up with an answer before the other person speaks. Be open to being surprised or learning something new when he or she speaks. Open your mind and your heart. Give up the steering wheel.

Listen. Listen—deeply, shutting out all other thoughts and impressions.

Cross. Solve the problem as best you can, even if it costs you. Trust that God gave you this person to listen to because He knew you had what it takes to do something about it.

Try it today. Or tomorrow. It will pleasantly surprise you how well it works. And it just might make a lasting difference in the life of another human being.

For him, what Dr. Randy Jacobs did was fairly simple. For me, it was life-changing. Perhaps—lifesaving.

Application and Discussion

* Practice listening to someone this week without even making a sound. Just use eye contact. Don't even nod. What did you learn by trying this?

* Walk through the *stop, look, listen, cross* pattern (applied to listening, above) and see if you can memorize it. Why does crossing too soon cause problems?

* Tell a story to yourself or others about the time in your life when you were best listened to. Imagine ways you can be that listening person for others. Is there any reason you can't practice this in the next few days, thereby becoming a big influence in a person's life?

* What do you think of the statement, "Listening is more influential than teaching, speaking, or preaching"?

Maintain Healthy Boundaries

Good fences make good neighbors. —Robert Frost[3]

All healthy cells in your body have a membrane, or boundary. Most of you lock your doors when you go to sleep at night.

Unfortunately, many people equate love with giving in whenever they have a conflict with someone, or worse, whenever they are abused. "Folding" all the time is just as problematic as trying to win every time. Both are interpersonal gutter balls on the bowling alley of life.

Passivity and weakness don't create love. They create codependency and people-pleasers who are drenched in fear that others won't like them.

The same Jesus who said "turn the other cheek"—which was never meant to be taken legalistically and universally, although this action is often wise and helpful in many situations—also

---

3   Frost, Robert. "Mending Wall." www.internal.org/Robert_Frost/Mending_Wall.

picked up a bullwhip and cleaned the money changers out of the temple.

For everything, there is a season. There is a time to let the authorities strike you over and over, as Gandhi did. There is also a season to set boundaries and push back.

I do not believe it is ever ethical to initiate violence; but using force to keep yourself or someone else from becoming the victim of initiated violence is often the most loving thing to do.

Jesus does not call us to be doormats, but to be noble servants of one another—and to serve with dignity, not like a dog that cowers because it has been hit one too many times.

Jesus was gentle when He needed to be gentle and forceful when He needed to be forceful. He was killed, after all, for His audacity, not for His meekness.

In fact, those of us who are strong should use that strength to protect the weak among us so that they, over time, can become strong.

Let the weak say, "I am strong." —Joel 3:10

There is no cosmic playbook. The Bible will give you the specific-situation discernment as to when to yield and when to resist, but we have to listen to the direct voice of God right now as things are happening.

And this is certainly possible, because Jesus tells us to listen to His (shepherd's) voice. He wouldn't say this if it were above our abilities.

But the time to fix the roof is not when the storm hits. Develop your listening capacity toward God when things are relaxed, not when they are in crisis.

Day-in, day-out cultivation of a solid relationship with God, speaking and especially listening to Him, isn't very sexy or exciting. It's hard work. And it takes discipline.

Don't try it out for the first time when you are in a threatening situation with others intimidating you.

The classic film, *Karate Kid*, has a long, boring segment we all know as the "wax on, wax off" scenes. Check it out on YouTube if you haven't seen it. A young boy has a karate coach, Mr. Miagi, who has several classic cars. The coach has him spend days waxing the cars with very specific repetitive movements. Boring.

But then the battle comes, the student responds immediately with all the right moves (which he learned while waxing the cars).

Battles will come in life. Are you committing to wax-on, wax-off discipline in your prayer life? It will make all the difference when the heat is on.

Application and Discussion

* How has avoiding conflict hurt the direction of your life?

* Do you have people in your life who continuously violate your boundaries? Name them in your mind. When would be the best time to start pushing back? "Never" is not a good option. Or is it?

* There is no single way to respond to a person who is trying to coerce you or force you to do or say something. Why is it essential that we cultivate a hotline with the Lord so that we are prepared to take direction when conflict heats up around us? What would you have to do to make this a reality?

Do the Right Thing

That other person is just not cooperating! My hands are tied!

Really?

In my experience, even in the worst of marriages, if just one of you wants to save it, it's usually possible.

In any human relationship between you and another person, you and the Lord form a majority. As the Bible says, "a threefold cord is not quickly broken" (Eccl. 4:12).

Every long-term relationship will have at least a few moments when system failure becomes a real possibility.

But these family and friend ties resemble a pension fund. You put deposits in week after week, for years. Each is a gold coin of quality time from your heart. Everyone gets the same amount of coins per year—time is an equal-opportunity employer.

Think of a long marriage, which goes for years or decades. It could well be that you have given over half of your relational-time coins to that one person; little pieces of your heart and soul.

For each coin you drop into the silver-slotted opening to his or her heart, you can hear it landing in the vaulted safe of your beloved's inner being.

You never get those coins back. Time rolls on in one direction. But that golden coin continues to add value to your relationship. Most of us have a few relationships that are literally priceless.

Say you have a huge blowout with your spouse of seven years. It appears that your problem may indeed loom larger than your relationship. In fact, things are so conflicted and uncomfortable, the thought of having him or her out of your life is a little bit tempting.

We may even start complaining to others about our spouse, hoping to get them on our side in the battle. Often we cheapen the word *abuse* (which can be a very real problem, but the word can be inflated and overused) by affixing it to our partner, in case we need justification for ending the relationship.

But wait.

How much have you invested in your spouse? How many gold coins are in the spiritual bank? If you walk away, you walk away from that investment.

Would you walk away from a fully-funded pension shortly before retirement? Would you walk away from a paid-off home, handing the keys to someone else? Of course not.

So why would you even consider forfeiting the most valuable investment you have, your primary relationship? Jesus tells us to "count the cost" before making a big decision (Luke 14:28).

Marriages especially, but also other high-value relationships, are so very costly to break. The emotional debt caused by companion-rupture forces many into the emotional red zone for the rest of their lives. Divorce is a social, financial, spiritual, and emotional smoking crater. Thus the Bible is clear in telling us that "God hates divorce" (Mal. 2:16). Not because He hates us, but because He wants to spare us the pain and the scars.

Perhaps almost half of you reading this are divorced. You know this pain. You can't go back and fix it, and "it is what it is." But you can resolve in your heart to do the right thing and fight for your primary relationships now and in the future.

You can't go the distance with everyone on the planet. But you can choose a handful of people in whom to deposit your precious golden coins of time and attention. Those are the ones about whom we say in our heart of hearts to ourselves: "Till death do us part." Friends. Family. Colleagues. As we say here in California, compadres and comadres.

Imperfect as they are, they are worth fighting for.

Remember, "And a threefold cord is not quickly broken" (Ecclesiastes 4:12).

These people are worth your investment. And you are worth theirs. Cherish them.

Application and Discussion

* Of course, actual abuse is never okay. But in what ways can the term *abuse* be misapplied? If you yell at someone in anger, is it appropriate for her to call it abuse in every instance? What are some of the downsides to affixing the *abuse* label to an overly broad definition of someone's words or actions?

* What are some signs, if any, that the culture of lifelong marriage and family is slipping away in your community?

* Why do you think people wouldn't dream of walking away from a fully-funded pension, but they would quite easily walk away from a lifetime of gold-coin investment in another person?

* How is it helpful to see relationships as precious investments?

Be Confident

The cover of a book once caught my attention: *No One Belongs Here More Than You.*

I have never read that little, colorful volume, but the title carries so very much gravity and wisdom. Many of us, perhaps especially in junior high, had the very normal and natural experience of not fitting in.

People don't like me and if they knew what I'm really like, they'd never want to be with me.

Rare is the man or the woman who has never thought that thought. Perhaps you still believe it.

But the simple truth is: no one belongs here more than you. You were created from scratch (there was zero *you* a year before you were born), and thrown into this world without your permission.

You reached your first or second birthday before you got a sense of your identity or even had a clue about your place in the scheme of things. Most likely, it took awhile before you understood that there was a reason that others were larger than you and that you would become one of these "grown-ups" someday.

But then you collided with your first forceful rejection from an individual or a group. They told you to go away. Perhaps you were puzzled at first; then the pain, upon realization, may have become visceral or even unbearable to you. Children can be unbelievably cruel to one another, and no one escapes toddlerhood unscathed. That experience echoes through the halls of your emotional memory, haunting you with the idea that you don't measure up and will have to make do in life . . . alone.

But you aren't in this alone. It happens to every single person!

Even Jesus got rejected—in a big way. Our self-worth does not come from our popularity poll numbers (which are usually higher than we think anyway). It comes from the simple fact that the Creator brought us forth and placed us here on purpose.

In fact, you won the cosmic lottery. We haven't found life anywhere outside of Earth (as of this writing), and only a tiny fraction of the mass of our planet and what's on it can be considered "alive." And most of that, grass, forests, kelp, and plankton, is hardly what we would call "conscious." Some higher animals, in my opinion, especially dogs, seem to have some emotional breadth and higher awareness.

But it is beyond all doubt that we are the very crown of creation. I can store my thoughts on this page, and your eyes will recreate images and ideas in your mind that match mine. I am sharing this with you through my fingertips on a keyboard. The shapes of the letters were designed by inscription carvers in an ancient city called Rome. The language was invented centuries ago near London. You could go to your phone and send a copy of this book to anyone on earth—most could have it in their hands in two days.

You eat an apple, and your body turns it into energy, which lights up your eyes and regulates hundreds of chemical and temperature levels—processes pulsing within your skin. Most humans fall in love with someone of the opposite sex and create new people that look like a blend of the two of them. The miracles go on and on . . .

But the greatest miracle of all is that the power and intelligence behind this fast universe, if you quiet your soul, is communicating with you. The Creator personally invites you to create with Him—to be a part of His grand project. Listen daily for that still, small voice. We are the gardeners and caretakers of this glorious, cloud-swirled orb we call Earth.

Reason enough to enter confidently into lasting and meaningful relationships with others?

You are the crown of creation. No one belongs here more than you.

Application and Discussion

* Describe a painful time when you felt unwelcome or unwanted.

* Name several ways people in our culture keep score of their own sense of self-worth. Which of them are the least healthy?

* Why do confident people seem to have more friends?

* How does heightened awareness of this dynamic (belonging) make it so much more important to let people know you are glad they are there with you?

Chapter Four

THE SECRET OF SPONTANEITY

People have never been so prosperous as today, but also they have never had less empty free time. Our schedules are crammed full of obligations and promises to keep. Advertising and promotion, in one form or another, has coaxed us into giving up the last of our money (and perhaps even funds we don't have yet) and the last few minutes of our time and attention. Our "have to bucket" has gotten much bigger than our "get to bucket."

Garrison Keillor jokes about a church called "Our Lady of Perpetual Responsibility." Seems like, over the past generation, all of us have become active members of this congregation.

And what suffers is a sense of joy and spontaneous living, a sense of freedom and real choices.

It seems like a spiritual life would be just one more "ought to." I ought to pray, read my Bible, and volunteer at church. And for this reason, church activity levels have dropped to the lowest point in my lifetime. Church seems optional, and people are looking for some breathing space.

But the spiritual path is the only escape from perpetual responsibility. Curious? Read on.

Use Boundaries to Create Your Playground

Most of the paths to freedom and joy are counterintuitive. Here's the first one: rules help.

There is no question that you felt some serious doubt reading that last phrase. But my brothers and I were raised in a home that was blessed with a tiny handful of don't-even-ever-think-about-it actions.

As far as I can remember, they were:

- Don't steal anything. Ever.
- Never cheat on your spouse.
- Get married and stay married.
- Pay your bills.
- Avoid social circles where people buy and sell illegal drugs.
- Men never hit women under any circumstances.
- We go to church on Sundays.
- No bad language in the house.

So we were a little boring. But it wasn't legalistic. As long as you kept to this unwritten constitution, there was quite a bit of forgiveness for everything else. The family was only disappointed if other rules were broken or big mistakes were made, as long as you treated the big eight like an electric third rail.

All three of us boys did the usual high-spirited teenage stuff, but if we didn't cross the lines on the main things, a sort of special favor floated over us—and we could feel it.

It created a sense of freedom. I would bet a large amount of money that neither my parents nor any of us three boys ever fudged these guidelines—to this very day. We didn't just talk about them—in fact we hardly ever did. We walked the talk.

And what's the result? Not one affair or divorce in all four marriages. We aren't in debt. We have never hit women. Our homes are reasonably peaceful. I don't think I have ever missed church just to "do something else."

Not that our lives were perfect. We had issues—just not those issues.

There is no doubt in my mind that having some no-fly zones from day one has created a reasonably easy life for all of us. And ironically, this has given us freedom to move on to other things, avoiding the drama and pain that come with going off the rails in one of these areas. So many of my friends, neighbors, and coworkers have been trapped for years because of a breakdown of basic values.

Speaking of rails. Can you imagine a freight train trying to cross an open field? It would basically get nowhere, if it could even go at all. But put it on sleek, steel rails and it can go up to 200 miles per hour with the right horsepower.

You may think that the train has less freedom, staying on its rails, but the opposite is true. The whole country is open to this train. The rails are the key to freedom-producing rules in life.

Why don't you and the people with whom you share your life pick a handful of norms and values and protect them with an iron-clad no-fly zone? They don't have to be the ones I grew up with. In fact, I'm not even sure they were intentional—they were just the organic values that flowed out of the principles by which my mother and father did life.

It's never too late to start. Have a look at God's top-ten list to get yourself thinking about what kinds of values would work best for you.

Would you rather take your freight train across an open field, or glide across the shiny high-speed rails in a TGV locomotive in France, where the only limiting factor is the horsepower of your engine?

For me, it's an easy choice. It may be tough at first; but soon, as with any habit, it will be effortless, natural, and easy.

Solid rails are the gateways to a life of growing freedom and joy. If you have a good rail system, you don't even have to steer. Haven't you always wanted to put the throttle down and see what you can do?

Application and Discussion

* If you have a moral no-fly zone, what does it look like?

* If it is different from what you grew up with, how is it different? Are you slipping, or did you improve on what your family of origin had for an ethical operating system?

* In what ways do moral rails inhibit our freedom? How do they enhance personal liberty?

* Later in the book we will discuss Psalm 119:45: "I will walk at liberty, for I seek Your precepts." How does this make you feel?

Experience the Power of Abiding

There's an old-fashioned word from the Bible, used mostly by John, which I love a great deal: *abiding*.

New Bible translations have tried to put it into more modern lingo, but words like *remain* don't do the job.

Abide remains *abide*.

It's a relational word. I can only picture *abiding* with another person or with the Lord. You can *remain* in a garage, but you can't *abide* there.

Abiding is so very countercultural. It hints of quantity (not just quality) time, and no one seems to have that anymore.

Abiding is relational because joy is relational. Even when you are by yourself in the wilderness for days on end, any joy you feel is springing up from inside your well from the Lord, as living water.

And this joy of the Lord is our strength. Time spent with the Lord starts the joy meter. We can't just live on occasional super-doses, trying to make up for a lack of abiding aptitude.

Here's a clue to growing in your ability to abide and receive joy from God: learn to abide with other people. We use the same muscle when we abide with the Lord. If you are bad at one you will be bad at the other. Good at one equals good at the other.

So if God is a bit new, abstract, or even foreign to you, pay attention to your next conversation with another person. How is your body language? Are you sending signals that you are in a hurry to leave? Ever notice that you can't, no matter how hard you try, hide looking at your watch? Your body language is telling the other person that you want out, and that is so easy for anyone to sense.

Lean into conversations. Be the last one to let go of a handshake or a hug. Turn your phone all the way off. Be more interested in listening than in sharing your opinion. Hey, you already know what *you* think—and you won't learn a thing by hogging the conversation.

Once you have practiced this for a while, shift the skills over to your relationship with God. Today my prayer life is focusing on beauty and skill: asking the Lord to help me focus more on those things that I do especially well with the least amount of effort. God wants us to use our gifts, and we waste our time and His, continuing to do the things we're not cut out to do. This prayer has been abiding in my relationship with the Lord all day. I try to keep my prayer focus on one main thing at a time rather than rushing through a list.

If I don't pray another prayer all day, this one will make a difference in my life, perhaps even permanently. I've been coming back to it since early this morning.

Abiding. It leads to a life that slows down, spiritually. As we slow our spirits down, our field of vision broadens. Our understanding deepens.

Have you ever been traveling so fast you miss your turn and have to go back to find the right street? When we are abiding, we don't even need our brakes. We coast and glide to a stop just before the switching station on those shiny rails we talked about in the last section.

Abiding: one of the secrets to freedom and choice, which in turn brings forth spontaneity and joy.

Application and Discussion

* Which people with whom you have shared your life are always leaning out of conversations?

* Which of them are usually leaning in?

* Who are the three people with whom you are the most comfortable just hanging out together?

* What simple, concrete steps can you take to get better at abiding?

Hear the Shepherd's Voice

I remember having a Thomas Brothers Map in the trunk of my car. Wherever I moved I had to buy a new one. Most of you have no idea what a Thomas Brothers Map even is because you are too young and are used to GPS.

Thomas Guides were big spiral notebooks made up of maps of a metropolitan area. (The well-used pages tended to fall out.) As you "drove off a page" you had to find the next page, which is not as easy as it sounds.

You also had to be good at giving, listening to, and memorizing directions. A lost art. These were temporary rules that we stored in our short-term memory till we reached our destinations.

People like me with a good sense of direction were helpful to have around. To this day, I have this sense. I know that I am facing southwest while typing this, without even having to think about it.

Then came CB radios, TomToms, and now, smartphones that guide you every step of the way. These save us all tons of time and mental energy. When they first came out, map programs were error prone and buggy, but now they are fairly flawless.

My sense of direction has atrophied. No one is impressed

with my former skill in this area. Virtually no one can give or remember directions anymore.

Apply this illustration to your life, if you would be so kind as to do so. The world is your field of work, play, and rest. The *Thomas Guides* are the rules you are to follow in getting to where you need to go. The map program with GPS is the guiding voice of the Shepherd, the Lord Himself.

Rules are great because they work, just like the bulky old map worked. But the apostle Paul says that this law (the rule book) is just a "guardian" or "tutor" to keep us safe until we upgrade to life in the Spirit (Gal. 3:24).

But you're better off with the *Thomas Guide* if you don't have access to GPS. If you haven't developed a knack for listening to God's voice, you will just get lost without the maps.

So this listening comes directly out of the abiding we were talking about in the last section. You can't listen if you aren't present with God. We spend way too much time out of earshot.

So, getting back to my prayers for today—I am hearing God saying that if I over-function in areas of life where I have little skill, then others will under-function in deference to me, and the result will be that something important won't get done. That failure will have a cascade of bad effects. So I am now asking the Lord to show me where I over-function in nonskilled tasks so I can stop doing those things and focus on things I do better.

My listening for everything God has to say on this is not yet complete—so I will need to abide a little more today to bring our prayer session to a good conclusion.

Jesus says, "I know My sheep, and am known by My own" (John 10:14). Why? Because they spent days and days together in the fields. Hearing and recognizing God is a direct effect of the amount of field time we have put in with Him. There really are no shortcuts.

So if we are going to move beyond the rules—which is a great start—and use the "Jesus GPS" to navigate our time on earth, we will have to come away with Him (in beautiful Hebrew "lek, lek-AH") and do some time.

The promise of a Spirit-led life is great. In fact, Paul says in his letter to the Galatians it leads to great freedom, because "if you are led by the Spirit, you are not under the law" (5:18).

Your spiritual *Thomas Guide* is a great start. But can you imagine the freedom of the open road if you learn to listen to the Spirit of Jesus?

Oh, the places you will go . . .

Application and Discussion

* Are you old enough to have made the shift from maps to GPS? How does this relate to our spiritual navigating with God? What parallels do you see here?

* How are getting lost on in an unknown city and being spiritually lost the same? How are they different?

* How does growing our ability to listen to other people enhance our ability to listen to God?

Dance with God

Life is a dance. A sublime way to describe it, eh?

I love going to weddings for many reasons. But watching the couple's first dance as husband and wife is usually quite touching.

Centuries of development have organically produced the stuff we see on *Dancing with the Stars*. Men tend to be stronger and taller than women. Women tend to be more perceptive and responsive. Thus when couples are dancing, men generally lead and women respond—this leads to the smoothest motion that fits the physiology most of men and women.

My wife, Wendy, and I enjoy swing dancing. The better we get at the moves and the more we listen to each other's bodies, the more freedom, joy, and spontaneity we experience—and the more choices and options we have on the dance floor.

When it comes to dancing with God, it is obvious that we are not leading. But so many of our prayers are "leading" prayers. We take the initiative and ask God to respond to our list of requests. This puts the Creator of the universe in a rather frustrating and awkward position. We even try to muster up more faith, thinking that if we can have enough of it, God will do what we say.

Truth is, faith makes a big difference, but when we are leading, our alignment with God is off and our dance is awkward.

The best things in life come, not when you strive for them and try to get God behind you, but rather when He surprises you with a leading move and you respond with "yes, Lord."

You see, His choreography is miles above whatever you had in mind for your life. Would we ask a ten-year-old to direct the Bolshoi Ballet? Of course not.

The five or six big breakthroughs in my life came out of nowhere. I never earned them or strove for them. Golden gates of opportunity opened, and I went for them. I responded to the Lord's prompting, and my life went to a whole new level.

I am sitting in Seal Beach, California, because of a phone call I got with a job offer some twelve or thirteen years ago. It was a stranger, and I answered the call while driving with my son near Des Moines on a freeway near my brother's house. None of it made any sense at the time, but in almost every way—financially, socially, spiritually, and physically—life took a big upgrade with the move. I would never have thought of or worked toward moving here. But the Lord led, and I responded.

How much time are you wasting striving? In fact, striving makes us crabby; and when we lack joy, we end up out of earshot when the Lord sends invitations.

Who knows how many invitations to freedom and joy we've missed because we were buried in fruitless work?

If your prayer life is limited to five minutes of rattling off a list of requests to God and then diving into a sea of endless tasks until you wear out later in the day, you could end up watching comedy reruns on your flat screen, eating fatty snacks, and wondering what happened to your life (and your waistline).

We have to put in time on the dance floor with God. Learning how He leads, with strength and gentleness. Training ourselves not to have to know exactly what is coming next or what the plan for tomorrow will be. "Tomorrow will worry about its own things," Jesus once said (Matt. 6:34). Can we stop thinking about the things we want Him to do for us, and focus on not missing our powerful and affirmative responses to His (often surprising) leading?

Giving up control of our lives on the dance floor with God is one of the secrets to freedom and joy.

Otherwise we end up stuck in a perpetual, juvenile, hokey

pokey dance. And wouldn't it be sad if the hokey pokey . . . is really what it's all about . . .?

Application and Discussion

* Be honest. Does the idea of dancing with God seem too frilly for you? How can you overcome that?

* Name several other things in life that are like a dance between two partners.

* What is the ratio of your prayer energy between asking God to do things (leading) and responding to His dance moves with you?

Follow the Holy Spirit

"We have not so much as heard whether there is a Holy Spirit" (Acts. 19:2). A group of believers in Ephesus were like deer in the headlights when Paul asked them about the third person of the Trinity.

For many of us who are churchgoers, the Holy Spirit lives somewhere in the Apostles' Creed—and He doesn't get out much. In fact, we have cuss words for God the Father and Jesus, but the Holy Spirit even gets left out of that . . .

There is a worry that if we pay too much attention to such—for some of us, strange—spiritual things, we'll end up like some religious nuts, bursting forth and singing in tongues in the produce section at the grocery store. And who wants that?

The trouble is, many of us in developed countries have over-intellectualized our faith and have lost touch with our spirituality. We think too much and spend way too little time cultivating our spiritual nature.

Part of that is our lack of a spiritual worldview. We tend to see everything in cause-and-effect, mechanistic, scientific terms. The idea of a Spirit being real and present seems optional at best to most of us.

But the Bible teaches that there is indeed a Holy Spirit and that He is a person—not just a thing or a vague force.

Thus we should give Him the correct pronoun and never refer to Him as an *it*. Imagine someone at a party inquiring of the whereabouts of one of your family members, and your answering "It's over there on the couch in the next room." Much less should we treat God's Holy Spirit as a thing.

The Holy Spirit was not invented in the New Testament. He was present with Elohim (God) and hovered over the face of the deep. He filled Bezalel, Gideon, Saul, and Isaiah with His presence deep in Old Testament times.

Much as the future Messiah was promised, so also was the special coming of the Holy Spirit in power, by the prophet Joel.

Pentecost was the day of fulfillment of that prophecy and thousands came to faith amid supernatural language miracles as the Holy Spirit descended on the disciples of Jesus like tongues of flame (Acts 2).

So Paul asks those believers in Ephesus: "Did you receive the Holy Spirit when you believed?" (Acts 19:2). What if he knocked on your door, you opened it, and he asked you the same question?

And our answers are not just about some correct theology;

they are about abiding with an invisible being who is (unlike Jesus) impossible to picture.

So where do you start? Well, the two languages of the Bible, Hebrew and Greek, both use the word holy *breath* for Spirit. In fact, in those two languages, the same word works for both—there is no separate term.

So I find breathing to be a good place to start when seeking the Holy Spirit's presence. After all, the book of Genesis says that God breathed into the clay and the man became a living being.

We also breathe in unison when we sing, and that's why singing often leads to spiritual experiences. It may well have happened to you at some point in time.

So breathing deeply and praying, "Come, Holy Spirit (Holy Breath)," is a great place to start.

Read the accounts of Spirit filling in the New Testament and recreate the basic conditions you find there. Ask people to lay hands on you and ask for the Holy Spirit to come in power.

The Bible promises an answer to this specific prayer. Jesus says to ask, seek, and knock, and you will get answers, you will find, and the door will be opened for you (Matt.7:7–8). Later in that passage, He promises: "how much more will your Father who is in heaven give good things to those who ask Him!" (v. 11).

So ask.

Application and Discussion

* People have comically commented that most Christians are "binitarians," leaving out the Holy Spirit. Why do you think He is so easy to neglect, even in churches?

* Have you ever prayed directly to the Holy Spirit? Ponder this or discuss it with others. What did it look and feel like?

* What do you think breathing, if anything, has to do with spiritual things?

Put Away Self-Consciousness and Social Fear

Self-consciousness corrodes God-consciousness.

Most of what we are talking about in this book relies on developing an abiding, deepening sense of the Lord's presence. Self-consciousness takes the spotlight off of God and others and puts it on us. Just look closely at the word itself!

In many churches we have the kids get up front and sing for us from time to time. Why is that so energizing for the congregation? Because children are less self-conscious. At least one of them will show you her belly button while singing. Another boy will wave wildly at his parents. They worship and praise God in ways we'd like to, but have lost that ability somewhere along the way.

Even Jesus says that we have to become as children if we want to walk in God's kingdom power. Kids are spiritual giants. Why? At least one factor is their uninhibited behavior and thought.

So where do all these "hibits" come from? Usually during adolescence. As our awareness of our surroundings grows in our preteens, we become painfully aware of our vulnerability. We see how dependent we are on the favor of others. This leads to over reflection and examination of everything we say and do, and, of course, how we look. Appearance, never given much thought a few years ago, gains ultimate importance.

To preteens going through this difficult emotional mountain pass, younger and older people appear pathetically unaware of themselves. The last thing preteens want is to be seen with their nerdy parents at the mall.

Most of us grow out of this narcissistic season of life, but self-consciousness tends to linger like a bad summer cold that just won't totally go away.

There is one question I like to ask myself when I feel this way. "Am I being harder on myself than I am on others?" And the answer is always a resounding "yes!" You and I can be our own worst critics.

Swimsuit season is starting as I sit here typing, and I live in a beach town. Magazine racks shout out: "We'll help you fix your figure flaws!" My wife confirms that shopping for a swimming suit is one of the gnarliest experiences most women go through as summer approaches.

But when you are trying on that swimsuit, looking in the mirror, ask yourself the questions, "Do I look as closely at others as I am looking at myself right now? Would I come down on others for how I look right now?" Of course you wouldn't. If you would, you need help beyond the scope of this book.

Being gracious with yourself is one of the best ways for you to overcome the nagging sting. Would I judge someone harshly who looks, talks, and acts as I do? You deserve as much grace as you give others.

And on top of that, self-consciousness actually makes you less popular. It sends out narcissistic vibes, which all too often are read by others as conceit on your part. The truth is, you are the exact opposite of stuck-up but that's exactly what you are telegraphing. Others react by avoiding you, which reinforces your self-conscious, low self-image. A vicious circle starts, and the RPMs can wreck your ability to experience joy.

But the most damaging side effect of self-consciousness is a stagnating or nonexistent spiritual relationship with God. We are too stuck on how we come across to others to get beyond ourselves and listen to the voice of the Creator.

So end this cycle of alienation from others and perceived distance from God. How? Be more gracious with yourself. Treat yourself as well as you treat others. Cut yourself some slack.

God thinks you're worth dying for. You are fearfully and wonderfully made, a miracle of biology and spirituality, full of dreams and visions. This self-graciousness will open up intimacy and friendship with others, and the heavens will start parting so that you can bask in the joy of the Lord.

Most of your self-consciousness can evaporate in just a few days. Just be nicer to you.

Application and Discussion

* What is the most embarrassed you've ever been? If it's not too painful, share with others a funny embarrassment story.

* Why do many church volunteers prefer working with children to being in charge of junior high ministry?

* Why do self-conscious people, mistakenly, often come across as conceited?

Stay Free

Freedom is your natural state of being. We were created free and equal. The American Declaration of Independence affirms, in soaring prose, that you were endowed by your Creator with the unalienable right of liberty (in addition to life and the pursuit of happiness).

No one can control your soul. Tyrants can fence you in with barbed wire or prison bars. But they can't make you think anything you don't want to think.

Our freedom was not given to us by any government. It was not "voted in" by some majority. The Bible says that "where the Spirit of the Lord is, there is liberty" (2 Cor. 3:17).

Liberty is your birthright. *Unalienable* means that, unlike property, it can't be sold, destroyed, or discarded. It is a part of your innermost being. If you were to have yourself locked up, your mind and soul would still be free.

So living freely is not something you attain or earn by works. It is your natural state in God's presence. We can lose track of it and live as though it isn't true—in a sense fall from it—but it is a gift given by the Creator to every human being.

A playful spontaneity with the Lord may just be the highest level of human existence. As we mentioned before, it is the chief aim of man to worship God and enjoy Him forever.

Psalm 119:45 exults that "And I will walk at liberty, for I seek Your precepts." This English word *precept* has deep Latin roots in *praeceptum*—literally, "taking ahead of time." The principles that guide things, like gravity and the speed of light.

Remember geometry class? We spent most of our time constructing proofs. Euclid, who invented geometry as we know it, reduced all thinking and reason to postulates/axioms and theorems. The former were not provable, just self-evident. The latter were guesses, which we turned into facts by starting with postulates and working toward theorems. Step-by-step. Precept-by-precept.

Euclid believed—and he has never been disproven—that every thought system (including science) is based on at least five or more postulates (precepts), which can be approached only by faith. These form the foundation for the construction of every thought system on earth, from political views to ideas for new pharmaceuticals. There is no "fact only" faith system. Faith is required within certain precepts.

So if you want to walk in liberty and joy, trusting precepts about God's power, design, goodness, and love for us is a great place to start. In addition, loving liberty is loving people, and not desiring to control them.

The Bible is a book written on just such a foundation. Thus the more time I spend with its writers (Isaiah, Paul, King David, Moses) the more their precepts become my precepts. A house "founded on the rock," as Jesus would say (Matt. 7:25).

And the more I walk in liberty and joy.

You can't think a single thought without choosing some postulates. Each requires some faith on your part. They are by definition impossible to prove, although they seem self-evident.

Why not choose the very best?

Application and Discussion

* How many of your personal precepts can you name? We all have them, at least subconsciously. Trying bringing them to

the surface and writing them down. On what faith statements do you build your worldview?

* If we are born free, why are so many people in bondage?

* Look at the tyrants of history, the Pharaohs and the Hitlers. Why do they fear freedom so much?

* In what ways is our country more free than in the past? In what ways are we less free?

Chapter Five

THE SECRET OF INVESTMENT

This secret has to do with self-discipline, which leads to investment in life (yours, others, your community).

There have been a handful of extremely disciplined societies in history, among them, the Romans and the Victorians, who ended up responsible for much of the civilizing going on in the planet during their eras of flourishing.

Obviously, we're not in such a time now. I don't mean to paint a grim picture, because I am an optimist and a lot of good things are happening in the world. But we are more decadent than disciplined. "Our hearts have grown fat" echoes down the halls of history and fits pretty well right here and right now.

Discipline is a form of social investment, and it benefits us along the way too.

So you and I will have to swim upstream to cultivate personal discipline during this sloppy generation in human history. It's been done before, so we can do it again. Here's how . . .

Keep Your Vows

Earlier in this book, I described a handful of no-fly zones to avoid in life. Let's look at them in a positive way—flipping the coin over, so to speak.

Positively speaking (no "thou shalt nots" in this segment), we are to meet our obligations. It's a matter of fulfilling our commitments and meeting our responsibilities.

Now as a child of this rather decadent age, you may be tempted to stop right here and watch sports or some singing contest on TV. But I invite you to continue on and see the benefits to you and to everyone of a promise-keeping life.

Let's talk about marriage, which amounts to living out a promise.

Keep your marriage vows. If you ever made such promises in public, you crafted a covenant with another person that is in force until one of you dies. With around 40–50 percent of marriages including at least one of the two partners deciding *not* to keep this promise, we have to wonder about our willpower and discipline as a society.

Marriage has never been easy. There are no "compatible" couples who have a perpetual waterslide of a marriage, shouting out joy and bliss all the way down.

But marriage is not even really about romantic love or emotion. "I have feelings for you" doesn't get you much mileage in life. It's about the public promise. I get so many people telling me they don't need a piece of paper (which is technically true) to have a relationship. But it's not about the paper; marriage is about the public promise, and needing and getting the blessing and support of those present. Those with whom you do life as a couple.

If 40–50 percent of mortgages were to fail, we'd rearrange the whole banking system. Why aren't we taking the staggering divorce numbers more seriously?

Every couple loses that loving feeling from time to time. But the public promise stays in effect in good times and in bad (for better or for worse).

Here's the big question. Is that promise bigger than your problems as a couple?

For those who stay married, the answer is yes.

My wife and I were married on a sleeting, cold evening in Tacoma, Washington, in 1982. We originally met in the outdoor recreation club of our college, and we have recently rediscovered the kinds of activities that first brought us together. I just got back from an overnight camping trip with her a few hours ago.

I was just as excited to drive off with her yesterday in our VW bus (with camping gear in the back) as I was when we did the same kinds of things with a VW Rabbit over three decades ago. Why? Because of feelings? No. Because of the promise that has held us together through thick and thin—and there has been a lot of both.

How can a promise do such things?

Because in front of 150 people, in candlelight, I told everyone, through vows, that Wendy is the one as long as we both shall live. She did the same toward me. This was tattooed in our souls that very day. So every day I don't just wake up to a woman named Wendy. I wake up to the woman of my promise. And that's who climbed into the VW bus with me yesterday.

Our song has always been the Art Garfunkel rendition of "I Only Have Eyes For You," which is like a soundtrack to the promise. We were up in the mountains a few weeks ago, staying in a friend's condo, and we went out to a piano bar in a magnificent resort lodge at our friend's recommendation. We got into a conversation with this gifted keyboardist during his break, and he asked us what "our song" was. His jazzy interpretation resonated through my whole being. The promise.

The marriage does not depend on the two of us. We depend on the promise, and we intend to keep it. And the promise keeps paying dividends of companionship, warmth, loyalty, and joy.

Application and Discussion

* What are some of the reasons, in your opinion, why so many marriages are at risk today?

* Why do you suppose there is such a lag in this new generation's willingness to get married and form families?

* Whether you are married or not, what can you do to support the marriages around you?

Take Responsibility in Life and Community

My wife and I were watching pelicans fly over us at the beach today. She showed me how they fly in a V-formation as they roam the coast, fishing for food.

One bird will take the lead at the point of the spear, until it tires and moves around to the back. Everyone takes a turn. The flock hunts and fishes together, veering off into elegant spiral dives straight down into the water—swallowing the fish whole before the poor victims know what hit them. They then circle up until they find formation again and move on down the coast.

It's beautiful watching the Creator's design in such powerful birds.

But I have noticed something about human beings over the

past few decades: fewer and fewer people are willing to fly at the front of the formation.

For instance, many churches have turned into big-box entertainment complexes where you can hide out for decades without being asked to serve or lead. And getting volunteers can be like pulling teeth.

I remember when I was a boy growing up in a little church in the mountains of Idaho. When someone died, the women of the church would fly in formation, like the pelicans, without so much as a word from the pastors or board. Meals for the family would be organized and delivered. A lunch would be put on after the funeral. It would all happen much as the pelicans fly and fish, naturally and organically. When someone got tired, she would circle around to the back and someone else would call the family to see what they needed for meals.

A mom in our congregation had a mental breakdown. By that afternoon, the congregation had removed the many children and housed them (for months) in loving families. One daughter stayed with us and even came on vacation to visit our grandparents.

It's sad to see how little of that pelican vibe is left in churches.

It's also hard to get volunteers for anything. And to invite people to fly up to the front of the V? Almost never get responses to that one, even in wonderful congregations like the one we are in right now.

Same for our local communities. We retreat into our little suburban mini-ranches, using our garage door openers and often not even knowing the names of our closest neighbors. Be responsible for people we don't even know? Let's see what I recorded on my DVR instead . . .

Part of it is a lack of joyful school spirit. Nations call this emotion patriotism. Now I'm not talking about chauvinism (e.g. My country is better than yours, so let's fight a lot of wars!). I'm talking about a simple loyalty and love for our church, community, and nation. Choosing to express joy, instead of just negativity and criticism, when they are mentioned.

Small *p* patriotism reminds us that the collective group—the pelican flock—has real value, not just in itself, but also directly to us as individuals.

Start praying for the Lord to give you a special joy for your church, your local community, and your nation. You don't have to agree with everything they say or do. You don't have to believe they are better than other communities. But they are your pelican flock.

We watched one pelican who had lost track of the flock. He was bookin' it to try to catch the others. Without them, he is less safe, secure, and valued. And his life may have less joy.

Stay with the flock. Contribute to the fishing flight of your pelican gang. From time to time, the lead bird will peel off and circle back behind you. At some point, there won't be anything ahead of you but sky (and rustling wings just aft).

Don't choke. Don't bail. Fly. And lead.

Application and Discussion

* Do you think that volunteering and leadership are things of the past, or are you optimistic that things can improve? Why or why not?

* Distinguish destructive patriotism from constructive patriotism. What is the difference?

✳ In what ways do people criticize their churches, community, and nation to give themselves an excuse for not getting involved?

Separate "Waste Time" from Rest and Recreation

"I'm just going to veg out in front of the TV tonight."

This is a bad idea for several reasons:

- You probably will take in almost as many calories (where are the chips and salsa?) as you did all day.
- You won't be conversing much with anyone, if at all. If someone is there sitting with you, are you really connected to them?
- There are some great shows on TV which grow your mind and expand your soul. Ever see them on top of the ratings? That's my point. A lot of the programming is just drivel.
- You are not a sports fan if you watch sports on TV. Sports fans actually play sports. Watching someone else play a game is not a huge problem. Letting sports become the emotional focus of your life is a problem.
- There is a slow slide toward questionable morals which will hurt your life in real ways if you watch a lot of TV. The programming is going to push you in an opposite direction from the vector of this book.

Much entertainment is just wasted time—neither recreation, nor celebration, nor (Sabbath) rest.

Re-creation (notice the word) heals us and builds us up. Exercise, painting, gardening, actively engaging the natural world, etc.

Celebration is partying. In a good way. Jesus seemed like He was traveling from party to party in parts of the Gospels. Some ethnicities are really good at this, gathering the whole clan around some barbecues and a soccer ball. But in general, we are losing our ability to celebrate on a regular basis with people around us. Older generations do it better than younger generations, who seem to have lost the knack for it. Small wonder that college kids lose themselves in a binge of partying when they go to college, having grown up with a celebration deficit.

Rest is commanded by God.

- Rest is not wasted time (trash TV and watching sports)
- Rest is not working
- Rest is not recreating
- Rest is not celebrating

Rest is rest. Unplugging. Learning to be at peace with yourself, God, and others without having to say or do something all the time. I firmly believe that much of the stress we are under, which leads to all kinds of disease, is caused by an almost total ignorance of how to rest.

The Bible says that the Sabbath (a day of rest) was made for man, not man for the Sabbath. It is the only day of the week that God takes so seriously He put it into his top-ten list, the Ten Commandments: "Remember the Sabbath day, to keep it holy" (Ex. 20:8).

When Wendy, my son Lars, and I lived in Germany, almost everything would shut down on a Sunday. Only gas stations and hospitals were open. Mowing your lawn or using power-tools was frowned upon. This hyper, busy, super productive nation coasted to a stop every week. This was back in the 1980s and it may have changed by now, but it was wonderful on so many levels. Resting was culturally supported.

While in graduate school, I took a strict Sabbath from Friday night to Saturday night (as the Jews do) since I have always worked on Sundays. Not a single book was cracked during this time, for four years. It was arguably the most productive time of my life. I firmly believe that you can get more work done in six days than in seven.

But most of us are totally unaccustomed to true rest. We become rest-less (notice the word).

It may take some time to cultivate the skill of rest. But if it weren't possible for us, God would not have commanded it in the first place. Even He took a day off after the world was created.

Resting for a Sabbath (one-seventh of the week) is much like tithing (giving one-tenth of your income). It forces you to trust God to take care of your productivity and your provision.

I know that when I break the Sabbath, it's often out of fear that God won't make up for the work I'm not doing. Sabbath-keeping, like tithing, is a spiritual discipline that grows our faith and power.

First of all, know what rest is and what rest isn't.

Once you have that figured out, you are halfway there.

All you have left is to yield to entering the Lord's rest. Every week.

Application and Discussion

* How comfortable are you with non-entertained, nonproductive rest? Describe any rest-lessness you experience in life.

 * Why do you suppose some people get so hung up on minor issues in the Bible, but totally ignore the idea of Sabbath rest?

 * What are two or three of your biggest, trashiest, time-wasting pleasures? Can you think of one to give up right away, and permanently? How can this be a substitute for true rest or recreation?

Keep Your Promises

We all think we keep our promises and are basically honest people. But psychologists tell us, probably accurately, that anxiety over keeping difficult promises may have caused our first-ever lies to our parents when we were little children.

So how can we become better at the discipline of making and keeping promises? We want to be people with legitimate reputations for honesty. Here are some tips to get you started:

 • Begin by resolving to be always on time for agreed meetings. It is one of the few promises that is measurable, so you will actually see progress and be encouraged by it. "I'll see you at 8:00" means 8:00. It doesn't mean 8:25. The Bible says that if God can trust us in little things then he will give us upgrades. Being on time is a physical way to keep a promise, and it honors those with whom you've made an agreement. It shows that you value their time. An easy first step to make.

 • Avoid the cop-out of making too few promises. You and I may, in our legalistic little minds, say to ourselves, "I'll never be a promise breaker if I simply never make a promise." We then can always come back with, "Well, I never specifically promised . . ." Little kids say that with a whiny voice. We are just better at spinning it. You can't be a promise keeper if you never make any promises, nor can you learn the discipline of keeping them.

- On the other hand, avoid making too many promises. Let's tell the truth to each other right now. Many of us have said yes to people, only to break our word later. Why did we say yes in the first place? To get the person off our back. To appease him or her. To say what the other one wanted us to say. We had no real intention of fulfilling the promise at all. Make only the promises you really intend to keep. It will take discipline to say no to people when they ask you to do something that you know just isn't going to happen.

- Recognize the exceptions. Never keep a promise when, in an unforeseen way, doing so will hurt people and/or you. "I've got to keep that promise" can get you in a lot of trouble. In the Bible, Jephthah made a foolish vow that probably cost the life of his daughter. Know when to bail. It's not very often you'll have to, but it's very important.

- Avoid overstating your promise. No need to "swear on a stack of Bibles." Many inflated vows are hiding a real problem. In fact, such dramatic gestures usually bring more doubt your way from others than confidence. As Jesus said: "Let your 'Yes' be 'Yes,' and your 'No,' 'No.' For whatever is more than these is from the evil one" (Matt. 5:37).

- Don't let lack of trust in people keep you from making covenants with them. Statistics show that people who trust strangers, giving them the benefit of the doubt, go further in life and make more money. Now if the person you trust turns on you, there is no obligation to trust him until he earns it back. You can totally forgive someone without having to trust her. Forgiveness depends on you. Reconciliation takes two to make it work. Trust? After someone breaks it, it's up to her to earn it back, not you. Thus you can forgive someone who has betrayed you without giving her your house and safe-deposit box key.

So cultivating a promise-keeping character (and the reputation that follows) takes some simple steps, starting with being on time and ending with trusting strangers.

You can do it. I promise.

Application and Discussion

* Tell a story about a lie you told as a child. What pressures tempted you to speak untruth?

* How can mistrust of strangers cost you a lot in life? In what ways is trusting strangers a good idea?

* What is the difference between forgiveness, reconciliation, and trust? How much control do you have over each?

Stay Physically Fit

Many have spent a lot of money on pieces of exercise equipment, which have become homes to spiders. We have become a soft and heavy nation. Sitting on my beach chair next to Wendy yesterday, we watched a whole cadre of women gathering for a big picnic, making many trips in front of us, hauling gear and food over the soft sand.

Most of them were around our age, and there were two types of bodies: fit and unfit. Since we were on the beach, it was harder for them to cover everything up with clever finesse. The fit women had a certain firmness in their ankles which traveled up their better-than-average posture, and their whole body mechanics looked like something that actually gets used once in a while. Their unfit sisters looked uncomfortable, with their awkward feet not really knowing what to do in the hard-going, powdery white sand as they huffed and puffed, dragging their coolers behind them.

Their basic activity level was easy to read on their very bodies.

It's really quite simple. We eat too much and we aren't active enough. The human body works best when it's slightly underfed and regularly under reasonable but strenuous physical challenges.

Which of the two groups do you want to spend your next decades in? Fit or unfit?

Much as we did with promise keeping, let's start small and build up. No radical starvation diets or gonzo exercise programs. The truth is, we all travel and eat out a lot—a monastic low-calorie regime cannot be maintained long-term.

- Stop snacking after dinner. This is the calorie bomb we don't think much about. In reality, we have transitioned into a society that now has four meals a day. That's about

1.5 too many. Being hungry is good. It's a sign you're burning fat.

- Split meals when eating out. It saves money and is the only defense against gargantuan portion sizes so common today. Feasting, a great joy in life, can be okay once in a while, but regular partaking of typical restaurant food can amount to having Thanksgiving a couple of times a day. If you eat out on a regular basis, you will get fat without taking drastic measures to cut your food intake. You would be shocked to learn the calorie count of a typical American restaurant breakfast combo. It's enough calories to cover most adults for an entire day. When traveling, limit yourself to one meal a day out. Buy groceries and snack for the other meals.

- Stop driving short distances. Get a good, solid, comfortable bike with fenders for the rain, a combination lock, and lights. With this equipment set-up, you'll be less likely to cheat and get in the car. I ride my bike almost every day, not for recreational exercise, but for transportation around downtown where I live. No need to worry about traffic and parking. Guests to my home are often surprised when we leave the house together to go out for dinner. They turn right toward the cars. I turn left to go downtown. "Are we going to walk?" they ask, in a puzzled voice. "Of course, it's only a few blocks." Next time you choose an apartment or a house, pick one within easy walking distance of a handful of destinations.

Forget about homes where you have to get in a car to go anywhere at all.

- Take the stairs. I visit a lot of hospitals for my work. Up to four stories, I always take the stairs both ways unless I have people with me. Same with parking garages. Climbing stairs works your biggest, strongest muscles in your lower body, burning the most calories. And don't buy a one-level house "for when we get old." Buy a house with a staircase so you will be forced to use it many times a day as you age.

- Eat food that resembles the stuff God actually makes for us. Walk into a convenience store and it's hard to recognize much of what is offered there as real food. From slushies to processed chips with artificial flavor. The less processed food is, the better it is for you. We are just beginning to understand the dozens of phytochemicals in apples and tomatoes, which are beneficial for us. Things you won't find in Pringles.

- Consider committing to an exercise class with a live teacher. Self-directed exercise, even with a gym membership, tends to taper off and disappear. And exercise DVDs end up in that drawer of stuff we never use anymore. We get busy and out of the habit. My wife goes to water aerobics and I go to (nasty challenging) Pilates classes, which feature a hundred different ways to do crunches. Could we exercise on our own? Sure. But a live professional teacher pushes us to do things we would be too lazy to do on our own. It costs more than a gym membership but is way less money than chronically unfit people spend on health care (type 2 diabetes, high blood pressure, joint problems, etc.). And if you pay for them, you are more likely to show up for them.

• Get outside more. There is no such thing as bad weather—just bad clothing. Sunlight is good for your spirits and your body. It's less comfortable than an air-conditioned room with a La-Z-Boy and a flat-screen TV, but that's the point. Your body has to work harder to maintain temperature outside, and this burns calories. Sweating on warm days flushes toxins from the body.

Remember the women at the beach: fit and unfit. Your body is a temple, and it gets better the more you use it.

Application and Discussion

* Have you ever noticed how lean everyone was in old movies? Compare the sight of today's children lined up during a school field trip at the zoo to what kids looked like when you were a fourth grader. What are two or three reasons that we have gotten so heavy as a society?

* What percentage of your calories is consumed after supper? Include beer and wine. Is this the healthiest food you eat all day?

* What would it look like in your life to double the amount of food that looks like something God made and to halve the amount of food that is processed? Be specific.

* What one physical activity do you especially enjoy? How can you do more of it?

Deal with Distraction

Time, unlike money, is an equal-opportunity employer. You and Bill Gates get the same number of seconds to spend every day. But in our distraction-rich society, nothing is harder to discipline than time management.

The whole world around us chirps, buzzes, and rings—trying to get our attention. Everyone seems to want something from us, all the time. Months go by and we never find the time for the important projects that need extended attention and focus.

The decades gallop by, each one faster than the one before, as if we are accelerating toward that inevitable wall of death at top speed. Isn't there a better way to slow things down along the way, so we can coast to a gentle *bump* at the end instead?

Some people are diagnosed with ADHD, but the truth is, our whole society suffers from attention deficit issues. As with fitness, there are some simple steps to take which help a lot. Let's start small:

- Wear a watch. The younger generation has abandoned watches for checking the time on a cell phone. What's wrong with that? The cell phone lock screen also tells us how many messages we have, along with other (not always helpful) reminders. Forty minutes later, intending only to check our watches, we have played Tetris on our phones, been entertained by Twitter feeds, looked at someone's pictures of her cat on Facebook, and checked the weather at our cousin's house in North Carolina. If you had worn a watch, you would have been back to what you were doing in five seconds instead of forty minutes.

- Disable notifications on your phone and computer. You don't need an alarm to go off every time someone texts or e-mails you. Check them on a scheduled and intentional basis. Control your communications—don't let communications control you.

- Plan by the week, not by the day. The week is a sacred space of time, given to us not by astronomy (days, months, years), but by the Bible, as a six-day task session followed by a day of rest. During the French Revolution, the leadership decided to go metric and switch to ten-day weeks to simplify the calendar. The people revolted and returned to seven[4]—it's built into our natural productivity rhythms. If you try to go through your whole to-do list every day you will go to bed defeated and frustrated with the things you did not get done; a week, on the other hand, can carry a lot of task freight. Doing this takes a weekly planning session and the discipline to make it work. We often overestimate what we can get done in a day, and underestimate what we can get done in a week. Then rest, and start over.

- You are not too busy to pray. If nothing else, prayer is an escape route. You need one of those emergency exits

---

4 The French Revolutionary Calendar: Wikipedia.org/wiki/French_Republican
   _Calendar.

with all the gravel and orange flags to stop your run-away-semitruck-going-downhill-on-a-mountain-pass of a day. Even if you aren't particularly spiritual, do it just for yourself. Breathe. Think. Get rebalanced.

- Avoid bricklaying. We can spend years in what I call ambitious bricklaying, the step-by-step attempt to get somewhere in life. It's the equivalent of working over-time in an hourly job to try to get rich. That never works. Ever met a wealthy person who got there by hourly over-time? No—they took advantage of breaks when they came. The same is true with time. We work and work at something, hoping for it to get big someday, and it never does. Chronic striving. Jesus explained that we shouldn't try to sit toward the head of the table (where we might get sent back down) but to sit, well-prepared, at the bot-tom ready to be called up. The key is to be in a good spiritual place, prepared for opportunities. Then, when they present themselves, you can seize them and capital-ize. Think about getting jobs. We've all heard about the people who sit at their computers sending out thousands of resumes and getting nowhere. And those who hap-pened to sit next to someone on a plane who gave them the break of their lives. I call this exhausting, petty striv-ing *bricklaying*. Be less ambitious in a striving way, but be more open to opportunities that may be way beyond anything you have dreamed of. And in the meantime, keep your promises, obligations, and duties. Pull your own weight, and develop your greatest personal gifts. Your time will come.

Application and Discussion

* What kinds of time management tools have worked for you? Which ones failed and why?

* How can striving and bricklaying seem like productive uses of your time but actually work against you?

* Consider buying a new watch or getting batteries/repairs for the ones you have. What would happen to your life if you checked your phone less often?

* What time of the week would be best for you to plan your whole upcoming week?

Protect the Weak and Less Fortunate

If you are strong, in any way, you were designed to be a protector. Children, those less fortunate, those who are vulnerable, and many of the elderly need your protection.

The strong among us have two paths they can travel: that of an abuser or that of a protector and provider. The less we focus on developing benevolent protectors in our communities, the more the strong will slip into a default abuser role.

We have become so egalitarian that we are hesitant to affirm the strong for their strength. All of us are equally valuable, but not all of us are equally strong.

This is not going to be politically correct, but it is true. Most abusers are men. However, we are less and less comfortable talking about male strength. The average man has 40 percent more upper body strength than his female counterpart. He is taller and has more weight to throw around. There are no women in American major league sports, not because of discrimination, but because they simply aren't physically strong enough to play in that arena. Downplaying this strength gap has led to a lack of guidance for what to do with this surplus male physical power. Thus some fathers, priests, and other predators find other outlets for it in destructive aggression. Not excusing it, just explaining it.

"I don't need a man's protection!" you may protest. Fine. I get that, and I affirm your value and strength as a woman. You may not need it, but many do. In the small town I grew up in, if a man mishandled his wife, the police chief would subtly let people know he was going to the other side of town and would not interfere with what was about to happen. The stronger men in town would go have a talk with the abuser in someone's backyard. We used to call this a back of the woodshed talk. It was an informal, but very effective intervention. I remember watching one through the thick pickets of a backyard fence. Strong male vernacular was used. The man would protest and get defensive, but he was silenced quickly by a surrounding maneuver. Seldom was physical violence needed. The message was clear. Keep your hands off of her, or we will stop you.

Strong women are also needed. They have been at the center of virtually every organized effort for social justice in our nation's history. Walk through any large, modern hospital or university. Often there is a picture, in a corridor near the plaques from the donors, of the founders. It's not uncommon to see about four women in an old black-and-white photo, standing in the mud among some tree stumps, one of them holding a shovel. The women, in long skirts and frilly shirts with hair piled up on top of their heads, are not smiling. They are staring right through you from a picture 150 years ago, and you do not want to get in their way. Health and education progress in this world would be unthinkable without such outrageously strong women.

We cannot abdicate care and protection of the less fortunate and weaker by outsourcing it to the government. Those who are strong need to take personal responsibility to ensure that all are fed, cared for, and protected. We have resorted to coercion (forced taxes) to provide care for people, when this should be voluntary. Service should be something that is woven into the very fabric of how we bring up children. Forced service lacks love. Voluntary service builds compassion and wisdom.

In the golden age of Amsterdam (the 1600s), the individual leaders in a small group of stratospherically rich citizens (you see them on the Dutch Masters' cigar boxes) would each compete to do more direct charity work than their colleagues. They erected and maintained some of the finest buildings in town as orphanages you can still tour today. They built charming little apartments for widows and poor women that encircle beautiful gardens.

You may say, "I am not one of the strong." But there is always someone weaker than you who needs your help. A baby. A toddler. A stroke victim in a nursing home. A disabled veteran.

And Jesus could not have been more clear: "Inasmuch as you did it to one of the least of these My brethren, you did it to Me" (Matt. 25:40).

Application and Discussion

* Why is this such a touchy topic? Why is male strength a taboo subject?

* In what ways are taxation and welfare an outsourcing of personal charity?

* The wealthiest people in your community, with a stroke of the pen, could wipe out poverty around you. What keeps this from happening in most cases?

* How can you shape the lives of young, strong people in your life so that they will grow up to be protectors and not abusers?

Chapter Six

THE SECRET OF ABUNDANCE

Abundance. Living beyond paycheck to paycheck. We all long for this, but sometimes we feel guilty asking for it, or we compartmentalize our prosperity in a drawer separate from our faith and spiritual life.

Somewhere inside, we've been given the impression that if we were to take Jesus seriously, we should probably give up the good job or the business we run, sell our home, liquidate our investments, and even perhaps take all of our cash, go down to the local homeless shelter, and divide it among the residents. What keeps us from doing that? Selfishness?

The truth is, if we all did that, the world economy would be vastly less productive, and we would all plunge together into crushing poverty and hunger.

You were created to be productive and generous. Get your game on. Get paid.

Help the Lord make the world go 'round.

Maintain an Abundance Mind-set

Mick Jagger was wrong.

His iconic song "You Can't Always Get What You Want" has

done more to promote and reinforce mediocrity, poverty, and scarcity than most people realize.

The Bible is clear (2 Cor. 9) that it's the Creator's plan for us to have more than we need—abundance—so that we can be givers, just like God.

Not just what we need. But more.

Not so we can hoard it or store it in barns, but so we can put it to work.

I once had coffee with a young man who was under functioning in life. He confided in me, in a genuine and heartfelt way, that he "didn't need much—just enough to get by."

I could hear Mick Jagger, in my imagination, singing in the background as he spoke.

You see, it sounds humble and spiritual to say "I'll take less." But what you are saying is "I want to participate on a minimal level in the lush abundance of this world, and I don't trust myself with the responsibility of overseeing more resources."

When I asked this young man, "Isn't that selfish of you?" and explained what I meant by that, he had a pivotal, life-changing moment. His family, leadership, and vocational life have gone through big upgrades ever since. I believe with all my heart that he is on the path to becoming a community leader someday.

We have been given dominion and guardianship over the vast bounty of this planet. But some of us would rather just be petty renters. Having a small economic footprint is truthfully just an abdication of authority and responsibility.

I want to be clear than I'm not advocating a "name it, claim it" form of ugly-American conspicuous consumption. The people I most admire have nice but modest homes and cars, and run honest companies with big payrolls providing for families, all the while giving generously to their favorite charities, churches, and causes.

You may say, "but Jesus was just a poor, humble carpenter." I don't believe that. All evidence points to the contrary:

- He was more accustomed to giving orders than taking them. He spoke with authority.
- He mentioned stonework over and over, never wood-work. Stonework was high-capital, high-overhead business. The original Greek word for his profession is *tekton*, best translated *builder*, and not *carpenter*.
- Nazareth was a short walk from one of the biggest stone-building sites in the region, Sepphoris. I've walked through the stone aqueducts in the ruins there.
- Some of his parables could be subtitled: "It's hard to get good help these days." He told these stories from the position of management, not labor.
- He talked about "the poor," not "we poor."
- His stepdad was of the royal Davidic family. His mother was closely related to the high priestly clan within the tribe of Levites.
- His family had enough money to visit the festivals in Jerusalem. A seven-day walk from Nazareth. That's six weeks off a year for three festivals—paying for food and lodging as they went.
- There is no evidence that Jesus ever needed to take an offering for His ministry, although He graciously received spontaneous gifts—such as the anointing of His feet with expensive oil.

Jesus was not a monk—He was a self-confident and an assertive, well-educated contractor-turned-teacher, from an important family. Paul was a tentmaker-turned-teacher—likely a supplier to the Roman army using skins from the Jerusalem temple—and a prominent Roman citizen. At the very least they were upper-middle class, perhaps higher in status.

Their primary thrust was into society, not out of it.

Over the centuries, scribes monasticized Jesus, turning Him into a twin of St. Francis of Assisi. You still see this in movies, with Jesus whittling away on a crooked little chair behind a shack of a home.

Is it time to put Mick Jagger out of your head and expand your vision of what the Lord might ask you to do for Him?

Application and Discussion

* Why do those who humbly produce and use less, seem more spiritual than others to many people?

* In what way does the description of Jesus in this segment surprise you?

* Have you ever been attracted to a less productive lifestyle? In what way could selfishness have been a part of that desire?

Become a Generator

You were designed to garden, in the broadest and best sense of the word. It was God's plan-A for humankind in the book of Genesis.

Look at these words:

- Genesis
- Generate
- Generator
- Generous
- Generation
- Re-generation

They share a common root, a depth meaning of *bringing forth*.

The Bible is clear that we are to be *generators* of value and abundance for all to share. One of the best ways to define work is adding value. The more value we add, the more prosperous society becomes.

Search the Bible up and down and you won't find the word *retirement*. Our responsibility to leave things better than we find them is the essence of gardening. We add value to the planet.

We help make the desert bloom. Look at a satellite picture of Israel from space. Ten times as many human beings have crowded into this area in the last century. The result? What used to be scrubby wasteland is now a lush, green postage stamp on the dry manila envelope of the Middle East. It is our nature to bring forth, channel, and cultivate life.

There are more trees in America than there were a hundred years ago. Part of this is because we have brought species from all around the world, adding to the biodiversity of our nation, making our forests more robust and resilient.

At its most bare essence, economic activity consists of taking materials we find, buy, or are given, and refashioning them into something more valuable—exchanging this, in turn, for credit on which to live or plow back into our business.

For a living, I draw from a gigantic education (which I was blessed to receive) and reapply the original-language ancient texts (the Bible) into forms that add value to the lives of people today. This entire book is nothing more and nothing less than that. You tell someone else about this book, and your action doubles its value to society.

It all comes down to finding a need out there, and filling it. If you are less creative, you just find someone who needs a worker. If you are more imaginative, you start a business to fill a need you find in society. So the free market is actually based on service. Whoever adds the most value for people gets the most profit. It's a way our society rewards the most productive among us.

Jesus said that if we want to be great, we need to be servants of all. That, my friend, He learned during His time in the business world.

Think of how communication has improved so much in the past generation. We can credit much of it to Bill Gates and Steve Jobs, who democratized information and communication by making it available to everyone. Their enterprises were rewarded handsomely for this service, and those resources are, to this very day, put to work by their companies, flowing through tens of thousands of our most creative minds—their employees.

I just drove by steel girders going up at what will become "Pacific City." Andrew Carnegie figured out how to perfect and mass-produce steel I-beams that virtually every builder could afford. This changed the face of human construction and how we build things. He made so much money (more than Gates or Jobs could dream of in current dollars) at a young age by adding this stupendous value, that he spent decades of his life trying to give it away by building libraries and concert halls everywhere he could . . .

The economy of the world is like a big electrical circuit. Add voltage to it. Don't just be a drain on the system. You will be blessed and you will bless others by doing so.

Application and Discussion

* People often retire these days for decades. How can these years best be used? What would be a total waste of retirement time?

* Distinguish between gaining wealth by theft or greed on one hand, and by acts of service and value-added on the other. How are they different?

* What is the one thing you have done that added the most voltage to the world's economic system?

Be Generous

Let's look at another *gen-* word, generosity.

It seems counterintuitive, but generosity builds more wealth than greed does.

When Wendy and I were going through premarital counseling back in the early 1980s, our pastor, the Rev. Cliff Ponnikas, suggested that we give away 10 percent of our income, and live off of 90 percent. I thought he was crazy. Between us we were making only $550 a month, working part-time jobs, and going to school. That $55 in monthly giving felt like a fortune at the time.

But he was so convincing that we decided to give it a shot. We've had some solid earning years in the early 2000s, but for the most part, high income has not been the highest priority for us. And abundance (more than we need) has followed us all the way through three-plus decades of marriage. We were able to write a check for a sizeable down payment on our first house in 1993, never having made, up until that point, $20,000 in a single year. We've never once had to take out a loan for a car.

How does that work? Giving 10 percent (also called tithing) is structured, intentional generosity. It forces you into abundance by living on less than your total income. And giving 10 percent in a disciplined way builds a sense of wealth and abundance in your soul. If you have enough to give away, then you start to feel abundant and even with lower income, rich. Every time you write a tithing check or make an electronic gift, it reinforces a self-identity of benevolence and prosperity within you.

We give our 10 percent to the church, but it really doesn't matter where you give it. It works for people of all religions or no religion. Mormons and many Hindus tithe, and are blessed by their generosity just like tithing Christians. It's like the law of gravity, which works for everyone. Generosity produces a feeling of abundance. A feeling of abundance creates actual abundance, because our circumstances, over time, tend to align with our character and temperament.

The greatest side-benefit of tithing specifically, or generosity in general, is an almost-shocking sense of God's presence. So where in the world does that come from, and what makes it happen?

Well, as we mention elsewhere in the book, God is a giver. Giving is not just what He does; it describes His very identity. In acts of generosity, we align with God's character. We are in step with Him. It is easy to communicate with anyone, or with the Lord, when we are in alignment with them.

So, if you are feeling distant from God, discipline yourself to a life of generosity and you will find yourself walking the same path as God Himself. In some ways, giving is one of the most Godlike things we can do.

Generosity also aligns our hearts with the objects of our giving. The Bible says that "where your treasure is, there your heart will be also" (Matt. 6:21). We start to invest our very selves into the causes that we support. This makes us more benevolent, and over time, less narcissistic and more socially attractive people.

I have been blessed, occasionally, to hang out with some seven-figures-a-year givers. They tend to seek each other out, and often sit on the boards of nonprofits, charities, and ministries. The networking reciprocity between these "benevolence friends" more than makes up for any money they give away. They trust each other with mutually profitable business deals because they know their partners to be givers with good characters.

Write some big checks, and you just might end up in some pretty amazing company.

But for now, consider tithing. There is no better or more direct path to abundance. Like a good pension fund, the results compound and multiply over time.

It will also force you out of consumer debt, which becomes an obstacle to tithing, as it complicates the equation. When you are paying interest, you end up trying to fill the bathtub while the drain is open. Debt is caused, not by living on 90 percent of what you make, but by living on over 100 percent of what you make. It's tougher to go from over 100 to under 100 than it is to start from scratch. With debt, moving to tithing requires a totally reworked mind-set. If you start tithing early in life, as we did, it can become a very real buffer against going into consumer debt in the first place.

Application and Discussion

* What two or three things keep people from practicing generosity in general or tithing in particular?

* Who is the most generous person you've ever met? What was most attractive thing about him or her?

* How would you advise someone to get out of debt so she could tithe? Should she wait with giving until she clears her debts?

Make the Most of Failures

I love to snowboard in the San Bernardino Mountains, which tower well over 8,000 feet above the Los Angeles basin where I live. Just starting out with this new obsession a few years ago, I was discussing with a stranger on the chairlift my first attempt at riding half-pipe. His advice as we headed up the snowy mountain was unforgettable: "If ya wanna learn pipe, ya gotta be willing to face-plant."

So very true in snowboarding—and in life.

We spend so much time trying to keep everyone happy and avoiding mistakes that we miss many great opportunities. Who wants to spend the rest of his or her life thinking "woulda, coulda, shoulda"?

So now, whenever I drop in on half-pipe, and I start getting too cautious and tentative, I tell myself, "I might just face-plant, and that's totally okay." The point of half-pipe is not to make as few mistakes as possible. If I wanted that, I would never do it in the first place. The purpose of half-pipe is to experience that couple of seconds of glorious weightlessness I feel on the "vert" before gravity pulls me back into the curve of what's called the transition.

The same is true of abundance. "I hope I don't lose money" is a straight path into a life of scarcity. In one of His parables, Jesus sternly rebukes the one who "was afraid, and went and hid [his] talent in the ground"—what he has buried is taken away from him and he is left with nothing (Matt. 25). Sure, we want to be careful and prudent with our resources, but "don't lose money" is a terrible mission statement for a business, a family, or an individual. It's like suiting up for the high school football team just hoping not to get hurt. At that point, you may as well not play at all. It's way safer.

Most of the wealthiest people I know have had at least one meltdown in life. The "smoking crater." A majority of them have experienced two or three. Their business fails, they declare bankruptcy, a trusted partner cheats them, a factory burns down, they run afoul of crippling regulation penalties, or they lose a big civil court case . . . The same is true in politics. Two of the most admired statesmen in the English-speaking world, Abraham Lincoln and Winston Churchill, suffered devastating face-plants over and over. All we remember are their victories.

Such generators usually bounce all the way back in less than two years. Their circumstances have not even dented their ability to produce value. That comes from a deeper place within them.

Wealthy people are willing to face-plant, because they think to themselves, "If I generated that wealth before, I can do it again—and this time better and faster, because I have become wiser over time." They understand how to offer service and add value, in a big way. They feel they belong among big producers, and this confidence gets them invited back into such circles. They trust their ability to generate.

I'm not suggesting you throw caution to the wind and do some crazy thing. Use common sense. Just don't dismiss big opportunities that come your way because of risk. One of the riskiest things you can do might just be to continue on the path you currently are traveling.

A bird in the hand is not always worth two in the bush. No one who thinks that way ever produced great wealth and value for our civilization or their families. Not worth two in the bush? There may be dozens of birds in the bush . . .

Failure is not fatal.

Application and Discussion

* Have you gotten more cautious as you get older? Some of that makes good sense, but what causes older people to become excessively careful to the extent that their worlds get very, very small?

* Tell the story of someone (perhaps even yourself) who came back from a large failure better than ever.

* In what area of life do you miss out on possible blessings because you go in with the attitude of "I hope I don't get hurt"?

Find True Rest

When Jesus greeted his disciples after His resurrection, it was with "Shalom Aleichem," or "peace be with you."

Israelis say *shalom* before they end their phone calls. Let's put that word under a microscope.

Peace is just a part of what the word means. *Shalom* actually carries three main components:

- Inner tranquility and peace with others
- Health, vitality and longevity—"La Chaim!" is a shout that means "to life!"
- Wealth and abundance

So if Jesus wants His followers to have all three of these things when He greets them with "shalom," then why are we so nervous talking about healing, and especially about prosperity, in Christian circles?

Certainly both can be taught to ridiculous excess. We've all seen the "pro wrestlers of Christianity" (some televangelists) who do exactly that. But why throw the baby out with the bathwater?

If God is a parent, and Jesus does indeed call Him *Father*, then would a good father here among us humans ever want his children to be sick or poor in order to depend on him more? Of course not—it's absurd. And I assume that our Heavenly Father longs, even more than our earthly parents, for us to do well and to thrive. He is not some sadistic Creator who set up creation as a torture chamber to build our character, to compel us to beg Him to escape the mess down here . . .

So for us to live a good life, we should keep peace, health, and abundance in balance.

Gaining wealth through greed robs us of peace with those around us. Striving too hard for money wrecks the health of millions. Focusing only on peace may help our health, but earning a living and enjoying abundance sometimes means getting out of the peaceful, comfortable bed and hitting the freeway.

Which of the three (peace, health, abundance) do you tend to neglect? For me, I have often neglected to cultivate peace, which has occasionally led to health problems. Cultivating peace seems decadent and indulgent when there is work to be done. But when I stop cultivating inner peace through prayer, then my joy disappears and my productivity and results drop. No one likes a crabby, overworked person. And they get way less done than they think.

Joy is the wellspring of all sustainable productivity. Joy is not dependent on our circumstances; it flows forth from the very substance of who we are as intentionally created beings. Once we are clear about our (God-sourced) identity, then our circumstances, good or bad, can never rob us of our deeper joy. Happiness, on the other hand, depends on what happens. Circumstances can affect our surface happiness. When the Bible asks us to set our hearts on things above, I believe that it means to affirm and reinforce our heavenly origin. This is the source of our joy, the anchor of our souls. We can lose our peace, health, and abundance if we hitch our star to our circumstances rather than the substance of our origin.

The Bible says we should prosper even as our soul prospers. Abundance starts from within. So how balanced is your soul?

Application and Discussion

* Which of the three corners of the shalom triangle is the weakest in your life? Peace, health, or abundance? How has this weakness affected the other two corners?

* How would you describe the difference between happiness and joy to someone who asked about it?

* A friend says to you: "God sent this cancer to me to teach me how to be dependent on Him." How would you respond?

Discard the Zero-Sum Game

So—what is a zero-sum game, why does it matter, and how do we escape it?

Think of a pizza. One hot, steaming, pepperoni pizza. Large.

Say there are five of you sharing it. Someone hands you the pizza cutter. You look around the table. Floyd, who played tackle for USC, needs more food than Betty, the eighty-nine-pound grandma. Floyd has a thigh that weighs more than Betty does.

How do you divvy it out? Even Stevens? Or by caloric need? By what they say they want? In any case, such a pizza is a zero-sum game. If one person gets a bigger slice, the others, or at least one of them, will get smaller slices by definition.

This is a classic zero-sum game. More for one means less for someone else.

You may have encountered it if your mom ever said to you at the dinner table as you looked down at your Brussels sprouts: "You'd better eat that—there are starving kids in Africa!" Of course, she was implying that somehow, you got some of their share, and if you don't eat it, that makes you an even worse person. You, agreeing that this must be a zero-sum game, replied cleverly with: "Then give these Brussels sprouts back to them!"

But the world economy is not a zero-sum game. Every time you add value to something when you could have done nothing instead, you literally grow the wealth of the world. The pizza gets bigger. Destroying valuable property or resources, on the other hand, through war or vandalism, shrinks the size of the pizza.

Attempts to divvy the pizza out evenly (as in Communism) have resulted in shrinking the pizza, because the incentive (profit) to produce better value is removed. Why should I work harder, or at all, if I get the same sized slice of pepperoni as the woman who runs a collective farm with 300 employees?

And such models tend to believe that the pizza will stay the same size. They never think about growing the pizza itself. And what expands the circumference of this hot, delightful, aromatic thing? One method has succeeded better than anything else: letting people, unencumbered and not appointed by the authorities, find needs and fill them. Doing acts of service for each other—providing goods or help—in return for credit. Then everyone is rewarded according to the value they add, and the more you grow the pizza's size, the more everyone gets. And you may earn more pizza than you can eat. If so, you can invest it in yet more pizza-growing, or just give it, out of benevolence, to those who have smaller sizes, or those unable to work at all (children, the elderly, the very ill, critically disabled, etc.). Benevolence raises goodwill, and the resulting joy also grows the pizza.

In essence, Jesus shows us in His parables that the kingdom

is like a seed that grows all by itself into something much bigger. God doesn't play a zero-sum game. In every apple are the seeds of a whole orchard. In every ear of corn lies the hidden potential of an amber-waving field of grain in the fall. In the seed of Abraham lay the genetic code for the Jewish and Arab peoples who now are thriving into the hundreds of millions of souls. God is not just into growing the pizza. He is in the pizza multiplication business. The name of the game for the Creator is multiplication. Jesus tells another parable where the master expected not just a percentage return on the silver he left behind, but a doubling of the wealth.

Stop trying to finagle someone else's pizza slice. Or hiring the government to get it for you through coercion and redistribution. Go out there and help grow the pizza by adding value to the world. As John F. Kennedy said: "Ask not what your country can do for you, but what you can do for your country."

This world is abundant. There is plenty for everyone who adds value through work. And the most productive among us make more than enough to ensure the well-being of the lives of those who are the least fortunate.

But for this to happen, we have to give up the zero-sum game and let people grow the pizza. What's your contribution to the world's abundance going to be this week?

Application and Discussion

* Someone is confused when you mention the term *zero-sum game*. How would you, without using a pizza as an illustration, describe it in a way he can understand?

* What can be done to keep politics from degenerating into "I'm voting for people who will get a bigger piece of pizza for people like me, at the expense of others"?

* Should the rich be taxed to ensure the least fortunate are cared for, or should we let the rich figure out how to give creatively and structure the benevolence themselves? Can we rely on their desire to give?

Think Kingdom

Jesus taught about the forgiveness of sins and eternal life. But it wasn't the tree trunk of His teaching. It was only a branch. An important branch, but a branch nonetheless.

The thrust of His message was the Good News of the kingdom. The Hebrews used the term *Malkuth*, or *rule*. Thus the *Malkuth ha-Shamayim* expresses *rule by Heaven*.

So, in essence, Jesus' parables and teaching, and by extension, His demonstrations of power were all centered in explaining where the heavenly, supernatural impulses (i.e., God) intersect the physical world. In other words, how does heaven rule earth?

A simple illustration of this is prayer. It's a spiritual, heavenly activity, the intention of which is to affect the physical world. In praying for your grandmother in Ohio who has been diagnosed with cancer, you are exercising this heavenly-into-physical pathway of the kingdom.

The Sermon on the Mount (Matt. 5–7) is arguably the most sublime of Jesus' teaching. In the very core of it (Matt. 6) lie the immortal words of the Lord's Prayer.

Look at the spirituality embedded in this heavenly jewel:

"Your kingdom come, your will be done on earth as it is in heaven" (v. 10).

The kingdom (*Malkuth*) is not primarily somewhere we go; it is that spiritual force behind all physical reality. We pray for it to *come*.

Until earth looks like heaven, we have work—spiritual and otherwise—to do. No matter what end-time opinions you hold, there can be no doubt, according to the book of Revelation, that we end up here, not "up there," on a renewed and restored earth. The pearly gates—present in so many St. Peter jokes about when we show up at the reception desk in heaven—come down to us, as the New Jerusalem descends, not the other way around.

So Jesus is trying to get us to notice and be more aware of this spiritual-physical hinge, where God's rule calls into being, directs like a symphony, and manipulates the physical realm.

But that is not all. He wants us to take part in God's work as partners. He is addicted, as the Rev. Michael Flynn says, to incarnation.[5] God loves to involve us in His work; it gives Him great joy. We are reality-creating machines wherever we go. Apparently, the Creator wants to deploy these self-aware beings, only if they freely choose to collaborate with Him, to garden and share dominion over everything.

Jesus' parables were all about this relentless, subtle, and somewhat hidden power of the kingdom, or God's Rule. He got very frustrated with His students when they did not have the faith to help channel and direct the power of the kingdom. "O you of little faith" sighed an exasperated Jesus on many occasions. He

---

5 See www.freshwindministries.org.

taught them that they could defy gravity by walking on water, heal the sick, create matter (feed 5,000 from a Happy Meal), and command mountains to move around. Occasionally they got it. But often they did not.

Jesus calls Himself the vine and us the branches, in John 15. If we abide in Him, we bear much fruit. The source of our very life and productivity flows from the Father, right through Jesus and into us. And it is not the vine that produces fruit, but the branches. We were created to be voluntary, not mechanical or forced—relational, self-aware extensions of His work. This same primary heavenly power that raised Jesus from the dead lives in us. Jesus called it *Malkuth*.

It's up to each of us to learn about it, recognize it, choose freely to say yes to it, trust it, and let it rip.

Until earth looks like heaven.

Application and Discussion

* You can go to church for decades and never hear much about the kingdom. Why do you suppose that is, if Jesus' main teaching is on precisely this?

* How much faith do you have that your spiritual prayers can have a real, measurable effect on healing physical disease? What, if anything, is holding you back? Would Jesus say to you, "O you of little faith"? Why or why not?

* Why do we obsess with sin-scorekeeping and forgiveness in our relationship with God and ignore our role as outlets of God's power in the lives around us? Is it narcissism, or misplaced humility? Or something else?

Chapter Seven

THE SECRET OF JOY

J oy runs much deeper than its cousin, happiness. The hurricanes of life can rip the spindly wooden beach house of happiness to shreds, but properly cultivated joy can weather almost any storm, like a solid stone fort poised for battle against the ocean.

Depression can be defined as a deficit, or even total absence, of abiding joy. In much the same way, darkness is just a lack of light; and water freezes when warmth is lacking.

Make Your Joy Complete

There is something satisfying about topping off the gas tank in my VW bus. It means that I can travel for over 400 miles from home. A giddy little feeling of independence manifests itself in a little smile.

Without refilling, I could reach my beloved Yosemite National Park, drive deep into the Mexican Baja, and toodle around the streets of Las Vegas, Phoenix, or even (almost!) San Francisco.

Topped off. Complete. The Bible talks about completed joy.

Let me help you picture this. The ancient people of the Bible such as King David, spoke and wrote Hebrew. This language had no tenses (past, present, future) as we know them in English.

Their two tenses were "imperfect" and "perfect," or incomplete and complete, respectively.

In other words, rather than talking about things that have happened or are going to happen, they saw them as either finished or unfinished. When Jesus said "it is finished" from the cross, He was expressing the completed sense of His ministry.

Faith is nothing more and nothing less than looking at incomplete, unfinished, imperfect things and seeing (through the eyes of belief) the same realities as complete, finished, and perfect. Hebrews, a fitting book for this topic, begins chapter 11 this way:

> *Now faith is the substance of things hoped for,*
> *the evidence of things not seen.*

For this reason, spoken affirmations, especially those with solid biblical foundation, have such power.

- I am a child of God; He delights in me.
- Through His wounds I am healed.
- I have the mind of Christ.
- I can do all things through Christ who strengthens me.
- Seek and I shall find.
- God has a plan for my hope-filled future.
- I am more than a conqueror through Christ.
- Nothing can separate me from the love of Christ.
- No one can snatch me out of the Father's hand.
- His eye is on the sparrow; so how much more will He provide for me?

- As far as the East is from the West, so far has the Lord removed my sins from me.
- With my faith I can move mountains.

Positive affirmations are often spoken out in the midst of incomplete, under-construction situations where there appears to be no evidence for a "finished" state of things appearing. Jesus used lots of "I am" statements, and He lived into them.

What is the address of your heart? Does it live in the completed promise or in the yet unsolved problem?

I am not asking you to deny your circumstances. I am asking you to consider not living there. Our citizenship is in hope, which is an anchor to the soul. I had a rough year in 2013. Many health problems (months of pneumonia), family struggles, care for an elderly relative who had a terrible accident, huge challenges at work. I lost track of my joy because I was focusing on my all-encompassing problems.

When 2014 rolled in, I decided it was going to be a good year. There was no evidence that it was any different than 2013, so I didn't wait for circumstances to improve before I spoke forth in faith "2014 is a good year!" on January 1. Every time someone asks me how I am doing (which happens most every day), instead of answering "fine," I declare "2014 is a good year," and I give the asker a hug. (This is California after all, and we hug a lot.) It took quite a few weeks, but soon my circumstances started to catch up with my faith. By May, some breakthroughs had happened.

Joy came back. And it wasn't a result of the improving circumstances. I simply chose it on January 1, despite a great deal of evidence to the contrary, and decided to live into it—letting my heart reside in the promise and not in the problems.

Completed joy is not something to achieve or strive after. It is a place to start, chosen by faith. Once chosen, you will sense your spiritual and emotional gas tank filling up. It may even overflow. "Today I choose joy" is one of the most powerful affirmations you can speak forth in the morning.

Joy is free for the taking. It is a gift of God. And like most good things, it is received by faith.

Application and Discussion

* Which three Bible-based affirmations could you choose to memorize and speak out every morning when you look at yourself in the mirror?

* How would you explain the Hebrew sense of "finished and unfinished" in place of "past, present, and future," to a stranger who asked you about it? How does this awaken you to the challenges in translating the majority of the Bible—which was written in Hebrew—into English?

* Find one area of your life where Hebrews 11:1 could empower you. What unfinished thing needs faith to reach a completed state?

* Have you ever memorized a faith statement about yourself? How would repeating it out loud on a regular basis affect your future?

Recognize Joy Stealers

When you park your car, unless you live in a small town or rural area, you lock it. The same goes for your home when you go to sleep at night. Why? Because you are setting up a boundary for those who would steal.

The Bible says that "the thief does not come except to steal, and to kill, and to destroy," but that Jesus comes to bring life to completed fullness (John 10:10). Followers of Abrahamic faiths have called this thief *Satan* or *the devil*.

I'm not saying you have to believe in a cartoonlike character with red skin, horns, and a pitchfork who is out to get you, but you don't have to live long into adulthood to perceive that evil often has a life of its own, and even a personality. It doesn't always behave as a disinterested force or just a lack of goodness. Evil isn't just a random pattern of a few bad choices and mistakes. It intends to steal from you. And like robbing the gold from the home lockbox, it seeks to steal the joy from your heart.

Robbing you of your joy takes the wind out of your emotional sails and steals your motivation and energy. That's your enemy's plan, and if he can succeed, he can take you out of the battle. You become a casualty and are no longer a factor in this world. He doesn't need to destroy you if he can immobilize you.

I'm typing this seated near the walking and bike path at Huntington State Beach. A steady stream of people passes by. I can tell in about two seconds which ones have been immobilized. Joy shows on the face, in the eyes, and in the vibe of the locomotion being used.

The Bible says we should always be ready to share the hope that others see in us. But what if there's nothing to see? Well, then they never ask and we never get to share the Good News. How long has it been since someone asked, "There's a lot of joy in you—where does it come from?" If there is joy in your heart, you might want to tell your face.

The biggest weapon in the enemy's joy-stealing arsenal is discouragement. He gives it potent emotional spice and cooks it up so well that some of us get addicted to it. Our language with others becomes one long, whiny parade of grievances. Like coffee or beer, which most children hate, discouragement is an acquired taste; but some of us learn to like it, and we use it as a way to demand attention and energy from others. We all know what it's like to get trapped next to a "griper" on a bus or an airplane. When one of them calls us on the phone, we put it on speaker, do light and quiet chores, and pretend to listen—with an occasional "uh huh" once in a while.

Constant complaining on our part is corrosive to our souls. Faith rusts away, and we become less and less socially attractive to others—causing loneliness, which gives us one more thing to complain about. Since discouragement is such a potent emotion, easily as addictive as cocaine or nicotine, we learn to enjoy it.

The best way to cure discouragement is to watch your language. Tell yourself you will not complain to anyone, verbally, today. Your tongue is like a rudder that steers the whole ship. Set your rudder firmly, and the ship will come around to meet it.

At first, you'll be shocked at how often you normally complain, because the urge to do so will be almost constant. What's sad is how grievance-oriented so many believers are. Some prayer meetings are nothing more and nothing less than gripe sessions with God. No wonder so few people want to attend them. There is less faith in many of them than in your average golf foursome.

The enemy destroys churches through complaining.

- I don't like the music. It's too loud. Too traditional. Too modern. Too showy.
- The pastor isn't very good. He/she should (fill in the blank) a lot more. I wonder if it's possible for us to force a resignation . . .
- I hate the Old Testament. Why don't we preach on something else this Sunday?
- Always announcements for the men's ministry? Why not equal time for my ministry?
- Where are all the people? Attendance used to be a lot higher when Pastor (fill in the blank) was here.
- Our board obviously doesn't care about missions/youth/hunger/children/etc.
- Fire the youth pastor. Always pizza and fun—never Bible study for the kids. And most of the kids in the group aren't even from this church.
- If they don't rearrange the budget, I'll stop giving.
- I heard that lots of people are really mad about (fill in the blank), and are probably going to leave the church.
- She always gets to sing. Why doesn't the director ever pick me? I deserve my turn.
- Our denomination is in error. We have to leave it.
- Something's broken? It must have been the youth. Let's put up a No Skateboarding sign.
- That church of immigrants that rents from us on Sunday afternoons always leaves a mess.
- I always have to do everything myself. You can never get volunteers anymore.

Church should be a place where joy is not only present, but it is amplified. Thus positive language should be guarded and protected.

So the first place to start, with groups or individuals, is with language. Ban grievance phrases from your grammar and vocabulary.

Slowly, you will feel the ship start to turn. Straight into the sunshine of joy.

Application and Discussion

* In what area of your life has discouragement caused the most damage?

* With what group of people (family, work, friends, school, church, etc.) do you spend the most time? How is the verbal climate? Mostly grievances? Mostly encouragement? How can you change the verbal culture of that group?

* What kind of negative speech would be the hardest for you to tame in your life? Cursing? Complaining? Gossip?

* Would you be as hard on others, verbally, as you are on yourself, in your thoughts? Think of ways you can treat yourself as well as you would treat others.

Slay the Dragon of Fear and Anxiety

Worry is a sin. The Bible commands us to have no anxiety about anything, but to bring our petitions to God with thanksgiving. Most of our worries show up in two ways: financial fear and/or social insecurity.

Money may not be the root of all evil (1 Timothy 6:10 says that the *love* of money is just that), but it does seem to be the root of all worry. This low-level anxiousness about our bottom line or net worth, even when deeply buried to the point we don't notice it, can drive many if not most of our big decisions and actions.

This happens to me when several capital purchases (air conditioner, water heater, furniture), big repairs (home or car), and other irregular large costs (travel expenses to visit a sick relative, etc.) show up all at one time. I am good enough at math to know that these expenses will decrease our net worth as a family, since we can't pay them out of regular income (which is for ongoing normal expenses, tithing, taxes, insurance). It feels like going backward when I know that at this point in my life I need to be building capital and not chipping away at it. This kind of headwind usually raises my anxiety level.

And it doesn't help that I know enough about economics and public policy to recognize the game that government plays with us, financially. In gambling terms, they are the house—and the house always wins. I'm not a conspiracy guy, and I believe our government usually means well. But I also know that inflation is intentional on their part; that it erodes our earnings, savings, and investments; and it enables the government to pay its debts back at a discount with cheaper money. It's a tax, an ongoing transfer of wealth, that most folks don't notice. Prices don't go up. The value of money, purposely and gradually, goes down. This could be one of those "ignorance is bliss" situations, and I may have even raised your anxiety level. Sorry about that.

But looking back, I see how the Creator has provided for me and my family every step of the way. And He who began a good work in us will bring it to completion. Has financial fear ever increased my net worth? Of course not. It's when I'm operating in joy that my income is the strongest.

The other primal fear shows itself in social insecurity. See if you can identify with any of these phrases:

- Are my adult children just nice to me because they want my inheritance? Do they subconsciously hope I will die?
- Why is that person always more powerful than I am when we are in a conversation? In the pecking order of life, am I near the bottom?
- Has my spouse ever cheated on me? I don't think so, but . . .
- What if that gossip in the break room is an attempt to get me fired?
- Am I masculine (or feminine) enough?
- My next job review is going to be another stress mess.
- I'm supposed to honor my parents but they drive me nuts.
- I wonder if there's something really unattractive about me, socially, that I'm totally unaware of?
- If I stopped calling my friends, which ones would keep calling me? Any of them?
- Why did no one laugh at my last joke? How do I recover from that before dinner?

When our tank is full of joy, there is no room for such thoughts. They are empty-gas-tank feelings that grow in a joy vacuum. Joy, when directed toward people, is called love. Will Rogers believed that he never met a man he didn't like. When we love out of an abundance of joy, rather than just out of duty or obligation, social insecurity vanishes like the morning fog on a hot summer day. When we love people, we aren't thinking about where we rank with them.

Joy brings financial abundance and loving, social thriving. Keep your tank topped off. All the time.

Application and Discussion

* What is your biggest financial fear? How does it drive your decisions? Does worry ever lead to windfalls of abundance and productivity? So why do we worry?

* What is your biggest social fear? See the list above if you need to prime the pump.

* Why is it so hard to feel genuine love for people at the same time we feel social anxiety among them? How does anxiety make us less loving?

Declare Guilt and Shame Bankruptcy

The cause of guilt and shame is simple. You are living in the past.

Now I could split hairs about the differences between guilt and shame, but these two emotions certainly are enmeshed with one another; and for the purposes of this chapter, I'll be using them interchangeably.

Unless you are right in the middle of an intentional sin while reading this (which isn't likely), guilt is all about the past.

Let me repeat for you a secret about the past. It doesn't exist. Sure, it seems very real in your memory; you may even dream about it in vivid and living color. But even if you were Bill Gates rich, you couldn't go there.

I hate to disappoint you science fiction fans, but time travel is never happening. You can't go somewhere that isn't . . . there. Now, perhaps we will someday be able to hibernate in some metal tube for centuries, awakening in the future, but that's as close as we're going to get to time travel. All things are possible, but revisiting the past is not one of those "all things." It's not a thing at all anymore. And the future doesn't exist until we get there and it becomes the present. One of my favorite signs of all time decorates a seafood place just south of here: "Free Crab Tomorrow!" See more on this back in chapter one in the section "Avoid the Gutters."

Guilt is based on the illusion that the past is still here. You regret something you are no longer doing. Your having committed adultery twenty years ago does not make you an adulterer. Having stolen your brother's twenty-dollar bill when you were in high school does not make you a thief. You are a human being living in the present, right now.

All that matters to God is your relationship with Him right now. Are you living a good moment? Here's another secret, God has already forgiven you for everything. It's you that doesn't get it. Sure, there may still be consequences for the mistakes you and I made in the past. A life of illegal drug use may have damaged your body. An attempt to cheat someone may have resulted in your losing a lawsuit.

But God is only interested in your present. In fact, Jesus warns us against thinking about tomorrow. Our relationship with God and others, this very day, is plenty to focus on—it's a full plate in itself.

We don't even have to remember all of our sins, confess all of our sins, repent of all of our sins, and promise never to do them again to earn God's forgiveness. In fact, the paralytic who was lowered through the roof to Jesus received a simple "Son, your sins are forgiven you" with none of the above list of qualifiers applying to the situation (Mark 2:5).

Keeping score of our past mistakes and bargaining this accounting with God is a game you will never win, and it distracts you from living a life of uprightness in the here and now.

Please hear me: confession and forgiveness can be very helpful and cleansing (1 John). Repentance (I've done lots of fifth steps with people in recovery) is a powerful character transformation tool. But if your spiritual life focuses more on guilt and shame for the past and not enough on your place in God's plan today, you are out of balance. The enemy will use guilt and shame to keep you out of the game. Because if your heart spends too much time in an imaginary past, you won't have anything left over for joy and power in the present.

So stop trying to pay off your past debts with God. Jesus already paid the entire bill. Declare guilt and shame bankruptcy, and start over with a fresh slate every day. "How can I live in holiness today?" is a question a lot more important to God than "How can I take that mark off my record from last Thursday?"

Guilt and shame also lead to a subtle form of narcissism. Of whom are you thinking when you revel in these emotions? Yourself. It's an excuse for obsessing over your inner machinations. And for escaping the demands of the present.

Five hundred years ago, Martin Luther was obsessing on his sins as an Augustinian monk in Germany. Basically, one of his mentors, tiring of the hours upon hours of Luther's confessions, basically told him to cut it out and get a life. One spiritual experience later, and Martin Luther moved squarely into the present, changing history as only a handful of humans have. He called this experience an embracing of the grace of God that is free and without asterisk.[6]

Two things happen when you focus on the past. You get old, defined as the past outweighing your present and future; and you lose spiritual power and joy. We can remember the past with fondness. But joy exists in only one place—the presence (note the root of the word!) of God.

Pull yourself into today. And do it today. Grace will abound and guilt and shame will wither away, atrophied by your lack of attention to them.

Application and Discussion

* A pastor gets up and leads a congregation in group confession and forgiveness of sins, and then says, "Your forgiveness is now up to date!" (I have actually seen this happen.) What's dangerous about what he said, if anything?

* How interested do you think God is in your past sins? Of course we are speculating when we pretend to understand the Creator fully, but what is your opinion?

* What two or three things can you do to live a life of uprightness and holiness today?

---

6   Martin Luther actually added the word "alone" to "faith" when he translated the Bible into German in order to clarify the obvious meaning of the biblical text in Romans 3:28. "So halten wir nun dafür, daß der Mensch gerecht werde ohne des Gesetzes Werke, **allein** durch den Glauben." (English: …alone through faith.). Luther Bible, 1545, Public domain.

* If we see sin as simply a bad habit that can be broken with practice, how does that help or hinder your getting free of it?

Forgive

Jesus was drop-dead serious about forgiveness. As I've said before and will explain in detail here, there are three components to this concept:

- Forgiveness
- Reconciliation
- Trust

It is so very important to keep them separate. Co-mingling them results in so much confusion.

Forgiveness is required. For everything. No matter what anyone does to you. You can tell if you've forgiven someone if you've stopped complaining about her and no longer feel negative emotions when she comes across your mind.

Otherwise, you have work to do. Forgiveness is not a requirement that earns you cosmic heavenly brownie points or some kind of a merit badge. Jesus requires it because it's good for us. You see, unforgiveness plugs up the channels of joy because our minds are clouded by grievances. Unforgiveness will immobilize you, spiritually speaking.

You cannot wait until the other party apologizes. The time to forgive is now. You and you alone are responsible for forgiving. "I need time," which sounds so reasonable, is also not an excuse. The wound will just fester for weeks on end, making you even sicker on the inside.

Sometimes we hang onto unforgiveness because it makes us

feel superior to the one who harmed us. That's often hard to let go of. God loves us as much as He loves you, and He always will.

Once you have forgiven someone, the next stage awaits—reconciliation. We should make every effort to reconcile when a relationship ruptures. It's important to listen to the Lord directly on this one, however. Sometimes it's important, for her own healing, for the other person to make the first move. Also, some relationships should not be reconciled. Some people are toxic for you or even physically dangerous for you to be around. To reconcile with a friend who became violent with you might be possible, but usually it's not a good thing to restore the friendship. Also, chasing after people who hate you may feed some distorted behavior on their part. In any case, the Lord will show you what to do. Jesus didn't pursue reconciliation with everyone who broke with Him or insulted Him. In most cases, reconciliation is a great idea. There is one problem, however; you can't be responsible for it entirely. The other person can always say no, but it's usually worth a try.

The third level is trust. Let's say your adult son steals from you to buy illegal drugs for a chronic addiction. You set up boundaries to protect your property, and then you forgive him. He asks for a house key, noticing that you've changed the locks. You refuse. He complains: "And you call yourself Christians and don't forgive your own son!" You counter with, "Yes we forgive you, we love you, and we always will. We'd like to reconcile with you, although that will take hard work on both our parts, but we don't owe you any trust right now. You've broken that trust and it's up to you to build it back over time—and then we'd be glad to get you a new house key. Building trust is up to the person who broke the trust. We love you and forgive you, but we don't trust you. That would be foolish on our part at this point."

So keeping forgiveness, reconciliation, and trust separate has a great by-product. It makes forgiveness easier when it's unencumbered by the other two components. It can be given immediately and without any conditions or requirements of the other person.

If joy is missing in your life, stop right now and examine yourself. Is there anyone you're still complaining about? Even just in your own interior dialogues? You don't even have to tell the person you are forgiving him. Because forgiveness is not really about him; it's about you. For heaven's sake, he may not even be alive anymore, or you may not even know where on earth he lives. It might even be a stranger you don't really know at all. It might be a public official you've never even met whose decision or policies damaged your finances. You might be mad at a whole ethnicity because of what one person did to you.

For the sake of the health of your soul, Jesus commands you to let it go. Today. Not just for the sake of obedience.

But rather so that your joy might grow back. *End result!*

Application and Discussion

* We've talked about forgiveness, reconciliation, and trust earlier in the book. What additional insight did you gather during this more extended discussion?

* Even though Jesus commands us to forgive, how can you let go of vague hurts from the past where you can't even really remember the details? Does forgiveness have to be specific, or can you just push the purge button?

* Chances are you still have reactive, angry feelings about some people. Who are they and what are you going to do about it?

* Would you be brave enough to write out a list of people you need to forgive in person, or otherwise?

Smell the Roses

My father-in-law, Bob, was one of my favorite people for many reasons. But one thing he said I'll never forget.

"I struggle off and on with chronic clinical depression. And one thing has helped more than all the medical care put together—stopping to smell the roses."

Now his native Holland is chock-full of flowers for most of the year, so that was easy for him at any given time. Most Dutch households buy fresh flowers at least once a week, if not more often. And they cost a fraction of what they do here in California.

But it doesn't have to be flowers, per se. A young man just parked next to me and got out of his car here at the beach. He walked, Red Bull in hand, over to a big concrete fire pit and strained upward on his toes to check out the waves. His perfect posture and eager face exude youth and anticipation. Not an ounce of extra fat on his body. He knows that the car he drove here (a rusty starter car) is just a step to getting the auto of his dreams someday.

He is not here to fulfill any obligation at all. He is enjoying every second of the very peak of his physical life. Walking back toward his car, he is in no hurry at all. As he drives off to find a better surf spot, you can hear that he needs a new muffler. He doesn't even hear it. He's thinking about the wave he's going to catch.

He's enjoying being alive and drinking in awareness of creation around him. And you just know that there are other young men within biking distance sitting in dark, smelly bedrooms full of dirty clothes and pizza boxes, lounging in front of computer screens, cursing to themselves while playing video games. They have no idea what a glorious day it is out here.

Smelling the roses is about intentionally enjoying God's creation. Getting outside. Learning to dress for whatever weather there is and enjoying each of the seasons. Giving up on complaining about the weather and just fitting in. Walt Whitman seemed to spend most of his life smelling the roses and "singing the body electric" as a vocation of sorts, almost never writing about being inside.

Screens will always be part of our lives, but make it a habit to look up. Often. I am composing this on my MacBook, but looking up, I see the desert sirocco offshore winds (we call them Santa Ana winds) spraying the top of the waves, just as they break, back out toward the ocean. The blow-dryer-like heat of the Santa Ana warms every corner of my body without the oppressive humidity that can come with summer. The bright white sand shimmers in the cloudless sun, creating mirage-like vibrations in the air above it that occasionally distorts my view of the water.

I have a State Parks pass hanging from my rearview mirror, which allows me access to some of the best "smell the roses" places on Earth. I never go three days without using it. I've rebuilt my VW bus so I can open the sliding side door and point the opening at the best view available. My friend Brent installed an electrical system that allows me to use AC current without draining the engine battery. Thus I have a mobile office, which I can park anywhere and sit out of the wind, my white roof protecting me from sunburn. How can you enhance and increase your outdoor rose-smelling time?

And the people around you are a physical part of nature too. When you hug the people you love, nuzzle your nose into their necks, and breathe deep the scent of their skin, promise yourself to remember each distinct fragrance. Could you tell these people apart blindfolded? Get over your fear of touching people. Of course there are good boundaries to be observed, but most everyone welcomes a hand on the back of the shoulder while you are talking. Never neglect hugging an older widow. It may be the only touch she gets all week. I learned that from my friend Tom before he died and have carried it out in his honor ever since.

The book of Ecclesiastes (which deals with the difficult dance between discouragement and joy) reminds us to enjoy eating and drinking as well. Ever since graduate school in Germany in the late 1980s, I've loved European bubbly mineral water. So a bottle of Gerolsteiner sits open next to me. I've been sipping on it for hours. I so enjoy my wife Wendy's home cooking. We had pulled pork last night, which I may never forget. We went out to a BBQ place in Seal Beach a few weeks ago and she said: "This was good, but I can do better than that, and for less money." And my-oh-my was she right.

Smelling the roses does not fix every little thing in your life, but it is a way of cultivating gratefulness—not for your circumstances, but for your very existence. And gratefulness, like salt on hot, fresh French fries, brings out the very flavor of joy.

Get outside today. And every chance you get.

Application and Discussion

* Try to find a way to read the rest of this book (or study it in a group) outside. Do you look forward to it or dread doing this outdoors? What does that tell you about your comfortableness with being out in creation?

* You are more likely to do things outside if you enjoy them. What outdoor activities are the most fun for you?

* What short list of people could you recognize by scent? How can you grow that list?

Cultivate a Sabbath Practice

"I don't need organized religion to be spiritual."

Yeah, yeah. Whatever.

You believe in organized education. Organized sports. Organized highway systems. But faith and spirituality has to be unintentional and random? Devoid of a lasting relational dynamic?

The truth is, a faith family can be a great source of joy. A congregation is not so much an intellectual pattern to which you subscribe. It is a real community of real people gathering in real time to build real relationships. In person.

When in history have we needed that more than right now?

I've used this word a lot in this book, and I'm going to use it one more time: intention. Cultivating our presence in our faith families, as a culture, has fallen to last place in our scale of *must have for life.*

intentionality. Behind youth volleyball and watching other people play sports on a screen. And whatever singing competition is on TV.

For all of its flaws (and I've written about them in this book), Christian community is, in my mind, the great hope of the human race. I can't speak from experience for most other religions, but I have seen some Jewish congregations that share some of the same qualities and benefits.

Voluntary spiritual community built around the reinforcement of shared positive values, mutual aid, the holistic and spiritual development of children, and the preservation and transmission of the best of ancient wisdom is a priceless asset to any nation or ethnicity. Elvis and Oprah developed the very skills that touched and influenced the whole world in little white churches (in need of paint) in rural Mississippi, not all that far from each other.

It was in a little brick church in the mountains of Idaho where I learned to socialize in a multigenerational setting, and memorized paragraph after paragraph of Thomas Cranmer (arguably one of the greatest lyricists ever to write in English) as his words came through in speech and song in our red hymnbook liturgy. *Wherefore we flee for refuge to thine infinite mercy, seeking and imploring thy good graces . . .* I learned to sing in four parts by imitating my father's father who had perfect pitch. Standing next to me, he always sang with a bass voice that rolled out with power, not volume, like a breaking wave.

The church basement smelled of potluck dinners, all the way into the mortar between the bricks. It was where, in grade school at the time, I saw an African-American traveling gospel singer break down, so moved by his own song, that he was unable to finish some lines about freedom. It was where the high school kids—wearing cutoffs, playing guitars barefoot, and returning from Bible camp at the height of the Jesus movement in the early 1970s—asked the pastor if they could have the service this week so they could teach us the songs they learned at camp. They told us that Jesus was their superstar, and gave us the eleventh commandment: "Don't sweat it." It was where our Native American custodian named Ham would clean the stained-glass windows with a toothbrush "to let the light in better." Every Sunday, he would light the candles at the beginning of the service with his Zippo from World War II. It was the church that welcomed their son Mike back after serving time for a felony.

There is no way our children and grandchildren can be given a greater gift than this—belonging in Christian community. The main thing I learned there was that there was a source of personal power bigger than any of us, or even all of us together. It was an imperfect little tribe, in a dying industrial town with a sputtering lead smelter, that had formed around the joy of a message from two thousand years ago. The high point of the church's year was at the sunrise service every Easter Sunday. The smell of breakfast, put on by the youth group, came up through the vents. My dad, the pastor, walked up the silent aisle. You could hear a pin drop. The lights were off. The sun came through Ham's windows. The black-veiled brass cross stood tall on the altar against the back wall. My father reached up, and (rather violently) ripped the veil off and proclaimed "Christ is Risen!" And just like every year, the joy of the Holy Spirit would descend on everyone present.

Joy is the ultimate motivator.
It drives a life fully lived.

Application and Discussion

* Why do you think churchgoing has dropped off so much in the past generation or two?

* What one thing would you have to change to take your commitment to being physically present in your faith family to the next level?

* Name three people who could benefit from the insights on joy found in this book. Write the names down here. Why is being a joy-spreader in itself a source of personal joy?

* In what ways are your habits not always in line with your intentions?

ACKNOWLEDGMENTS

Every book is a group project, and the truth is, no humans have truly original thoughts. We just re-blend and re-present things in new ways. So I have a lot of people to thank.

So . . . I'd like to thank the Garborgs, most all of them, for hatching the idea for this book four years ago and not letting it go. Rolf, Mary, Joanie, and especially Carlton. Jason Rovenstine is only married into the Garborgs, but he was there at the beginning too. And his wife Lisa, a chiropractor and a genetic Garborg, who adjusted my neck at a family dinner for which I am still grateful.

Thanks to David Sluka, who along with Carlton formed the troika that actually put this book in your hands. Thanks to Jocelyn Bailey, Wendy Housholder, and David Sluka, my proofreaders. Wendy read the first chapters of the book and encouraged me to go the distance.

Thanks to my physical trainers Katherine Slay and Shay Haghighat who have changed what I think is physically possible and have helped me get substantially stronger and more flexible with age. Plus, they make the world's gnarliest workouts a lot of fun.

I am grateful to my friends Bruce Gera and BT (Brian Taylor) who keep teaching me to surf better. Bringing out the best in people is what this book is all about.

Blessings on fellow Stammtisch Kameraden, Bob Rognlien, Dana Hanson, and Steve Goodwin. Dana, this is my fourth book. Where is yours?

Thanks to my longtime prayer partner the Rev. Walter A. Jackson III and compadres Steve Zeeman and Brooks Larson for putting up with a less-enlightened side of me than the more helpful side of me that wrote this book.

Thanks to our couples' group, which has met for over ten years. There is not a single topic in this book that doesn't have some chain to an anchor in one of our discussions on Monday nights. Lou and Pam Mannone. Robert and Jewell Coffman. Tim and Vicki Scanlon. The most nondisposable relationships we have.

Thanks to Brent Larson, my mechanic, who keeps Red Rover (my '71 VW Bus) running so that I can go to cool places and write this stuff. I wrote most of this book outdoors. Not sure why there even is an indoors in Southern California.

Thanks to my mom, Delphine, who is better at selling books than Amazon. And to Jennifer Clark Tinker, editor of *Life & Liberty*, and to Lindsey Trego, my personal assistant, who do more to promote my ideas than I ever could. Lindsey also frees up my time to be creative by managing most everything I do. Unfortunately, I can be somewhat calendrically challenged.

This book has a lot to say about forgiveness, and my son Lars (born 1988) embodies that by virtually never having held a grudge.

Thanks to the folks at Robinwood Church in Orange County, California, for giving me the chance to teach on these ideas every Sunday at 10:30 a.m. and for going the distance with me, all the time. Special mention to Bud Potter, John Ellis, and LeRoy Wood who, every Monday morning over breakfast, help me write my sermons. Teams are smarter than people.

Avivah Zornberg of Israel and Eugen Drewermann of Germany are Bible teachers whose thoughts, at least indirectly, permeate much of what I teach and write. Ditto, the evangelist we know as Mark; that cool guy who wrote one of the four Gospels and, in my opinion, did a better job than the other three.

Blessings on Dean Truitt, my faithful business partner and co-creator of The BlackberryBush Course, which your church needs to start running. Many of the ideas in this book come from my teaching in the course. www.BlackberryBush.org.

Special thanks to J.E. Danielson, Tom Housholder, Richard Dunn, and Bob Vermeer, all who are at home with their Maker, who embodied virtually every idea in this book

It takes a village to write a book.